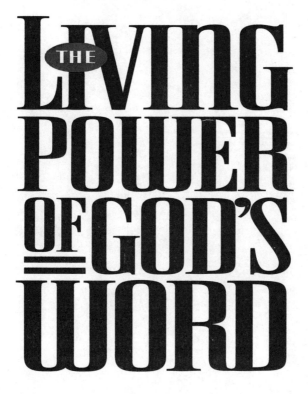

Stories of Unshakable Faith to Renew
Your Christian Commitment

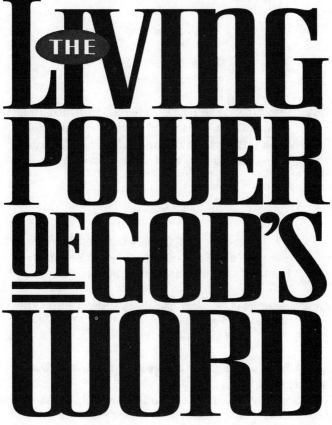

THE LIVING POWER OF GOD'S WORD

Dennis M. Mulder with Mark Cutshall

BROADMAN
&HOLMAN
PUBLISHERS

Nashville, Tennessee

Published by Broadman & Holman Publishers, Nashville, Tennessee
Acquisitions & Development Editor: John Landers
Design and Typography: TF Designs, Mt. Juliet, Tennessee
Printed in the United States of America

4260-80
0-8054-6080-2

Dewey Decimal Classification: 248.4
Subject Heading: CHRISTIAN LIFE \ BIBLE—STUDY
Library of Congress Card Catalog Number: 96-1078

Unless otherwise noted, Scripture quotations are from the Holy Bible, New
International Version, copyright © 1973, 1978, 1984
by International Bible Society.

Library of Congress Cataloging-in-Publication Data
Mulder, Dennis M.
    The living power of God's Word : stories of unshakable faith to renew
your Christian commitment / Dennis M. Mulder with Mark Cutshall.
        p.   cm.
    ISBN 0-8054-6080-2 (pbk.)
    1. Bible—Devotional use. 2. Christian biography. 3. Bible—Influence.
4. Christian life—Baptist authors. I. Cutshall, Mark. II. Title.
    BS617.8.M85   1996
    209'.2'2—dc20
    [B]
                                                        96-1078
                                                        CIP

96 97 98 99 00 5 4 3 2 1

Contents

Introduction

Let the word of Christ dwell in you richly.

Colossians 3:16, KJV

It was the one gift he never expected to receive.

On Christmas Day Bruce Hurt already had everything he wanted: a loving family, a large home, a successful practice as a physician at one of Austin's top medical centers, good friends, and financial security.

Marty, his wife, reached under the Christmas tree, picked up the last remaining present, and handed it to her husband.

"This is to you, from me," she said.

Bruce tore off the green-and-gold wrapping paper and carefully removed the lid.

"What's this?" he asked. In his hands was a brown leather cover imprinted with the words, "New International Version Study Bible."

He stared at the cover and then gently closed the lid.

"Thank you, Honey," he said. Bruce didn't say what he was really thinking: *What am I going to do with this? I don't understand the Bible. I don't have time to read the Bible. Even if I did, I wouldn't know where to start.*

Do Bruce Hurt's words hit close to home?

Do you wonder how, or when, you'll ever fit the Bible into your already overcrowded life?

Do you find yourself somehow not finding (or making) the time to sit down and read a chapter or two?

Do you remember when it wasn't this way? Do you remember the first time the Bible really came to life, when reading and studying Scripture was something you looked forward to?

How long has it been since you felt like that?

How long has it been since you enjoyed reading a favorite psalm, a parable, or story of Jesus? Or how long has it been since you explored a new passage and learned something new, something exciting about God?

Do you wish you could experience that same enjoyment, again, for God's Word? Do you wish you could renew your appreciation and understanding of this unique book that speaks directly to the challenges and issues you face every day?

Do you wish you could love God and His Word in a new way?

If these are your questions, then this book may hold answers. Because of the true stories and timeless principles contained in the nine short chapters, your relationship with God, your attitude toward the Bible, *your life*, could change significantly in the next twenty-eight days. Before I tell you how this can happen, let me share a bit of my own story.

My Life and the Bible

Unlike Bruce Hurt, there was never a day when I didn't know the Bible. I was born into a Minnesota farm family that prayed before every meal, sought the Lord's direction and protection, and constantly turned to the Scriptures for daily direction and strength. Today, in my mid-fifties, I thank God for this heritage. While growing up, I didn't know that the Bible would be such a pivotal force in shaping my life.

My family's devotion to God and His Word seeped into my character and guided my life's calling. After years of Bible training, I invested nearly two decades in teaching, training, and evangelism overseas. During this time I realized a foundational truth: *The Bible is God's one, constant, perfect, and permanent source of Truth.* While I gave thanks that God speaks through answered prayer and intervenes in life's circumstances, it became more and more clear to me that *the way* people could know the Lord and His good and perfect will for our lives was through the perfect revelation of Himself—His holy, written Word.

Because of this fact I couldn't escape two conclusions: First, if Christians, like me, wanted to deepen and renew their love for God, they needed to know this one-of-a-kind source of God's purpose and plan for their lives.

Second, and even more striking, was that people who had never heard or known about God and His Word were missing out on the greatest message of all time.

These two observations came together at a crossroads in my life that eventually led me to write the book you're now reading. In 1976 I joined the Bible League, an international ministry whose sole purpose is to provide Scriptures to people around the world who don't yet know Jesus Christ. The League fulfills this mission by partnering with churches and mission organizations whose leaders bring the Word to life in their own countries.

While I gave myself totally to this vision, I never expected to become the Bible League's president in 1985.

I certainly never imagined that the extraordinary stories of people I met around the world could speak so directly and powerfully to the needs of Christians on my side of the world. I never imagined that these men and women, so new to the Word, could offer such simple, yet practical, profound truths about Scripture to Christians who've known the Bible for years. Yet this is exactly what happened.

The individuals you'll meet in the next nine chapters are everyday people I've either known personally or whose life stories I've heard through witnesses who could not keep silent. One thing distinguishes them from you and me: they live in countries where the Bible is either outlawed or almost impossible to obtain. Therefore, these believers have the "luxury" of not being able to take the Word for granted. To them, a book from God that reveals unconditional love and the hope of eternal life is the most precious discovery in life. As their faith, their joy, their love for God and His Word become obvious, you may find yourself thinking what I did: this is what it means to know and love God's Word for the first time.

In fact, each time I've either met with or contacted one of these vibrant Christians and felt their newfound love for the Word, two things have happened. The first is that I've thought about my own life. I've realized how, over the years, my own desire to know the Scriptures has waned. I think of how lazy or indifferent I've been in spending time in God's Word. I think of how often I've wanted to receive more from the Bible—and how little I've been willing to give.

The second thing that's happened to me, however, is even more convicting. Today, the extraordinary people in this book have motivated me to reclaim the Scriptures for myself. Their stories of the Bible's life-changing power have helped renew my love for God and His Word and see it for what it truly is—not merely the greatest guide for living, but life itself.

The result is that, today, familiar passages I've skimmed over for years have come alive with new meaning, power, and relevance. Passages I used to pass over have become the source of new appreciation and new understanding for who God is and what He's doing in my world. In a very real way, my renewed encounter with the Scriptures has mirrored the lives of the people you'll read about. Today, when I sit down and spend time in God's Word I feel as if I'm reading it for the first time!

I believe the same potentially life-changing discovery awaits you in these pages. I want to introduce you to the ordinary men and women whose everyday faith can renew your love for God and His Word. These are men and women whose fresh approach to Scripture can speak to the obstacles that may now be keeping you from experiencing the power and wisdom of God's Word.

CHAPTER ONE

Changed by The Word

How The Bible Can Give You New Reason for Living

———— ∞ ————

"Be strong and courageous. Do not be terrified; do not be discouraged, for the Lord your God will be with you wherever you go."

Joshua 1:9

"The harvest is plentiful but the workers are few. Ask the Lord of the harvest, therefore, to send out workers into his harvest field."

Matthew 9:37–38

Santos Galan lives in Mexico City where he serves as the director of La Liga Biblica, the sister organization of the Bible League. Today, in his mid-sixties, he oversees the distribution of thousands of Scriptures to churches throughout Mexico.

When he speaks, the raspiness in his voice is immediately noticeable. For years Santos preached at hundreds of open-air evangelistic gatherings without the aid of a sound system. Eventually, throat problems forced him to give up his dream of being an evangelist, so he turned to spreading the written Word. What happened in Santos's life over the next twenty-five years illustrates a foundational truth of Scripture that underlies all the stories in this book: When God's love, perfectly explained in the Word, is powerfully demonstrated, both the givers and the recipients of His truth discover a new reason to live. The collective result of these changed individuals is a community changed by the living out of biblical truths.

This is how one person's changed life led to the transformation of an entire town, because a book that was once absent and irrelevant suddenly became real.

The End in Sight . . .

Santos Galan staggered up the first few steps. He breathed a sigh of relief; just six more flights of stairs remained. He could make that and then relax because, once inside his room, he planned to kill himself.

His untied shoe found the next step. His hand reached for the railing and missed.

All the wine and reckless years had now caught up to him. He could force himself up the stairs one more time. For years he had stood at the bottom looking up at life.

"I was one of five Mexican children. I grew up in East Los Angeles. Poor area. Poor family. Poor way to live."

He found the first landing, looked back down the steps, and kept walking. The walls in front of him grew narrow and dim.

"Most of my friends only got as far as junior high. A teacher once told me, 'If you were a serious person, you could go further; but first you need to think of your own self.' I looked at her and said, 'Drop dead.' That's when I dropped out.

"Drugs and gangs became my life. I loved to fight. With my fists, a bat, a piece of pipe. I got sent to jail, once, twice, before I lost track."

One foot in front of the next. He didn't have much farther to go. The end was in sight.

"I saw the winos sitting on the sidewalks on California Avenue. I saw their swollen, ragged faces. I said to myself,

'That could be you, Santos.' I thought I had the willpower to stop hurting myself. I was wrong."

Santos felt the door handle, felt the key give way, then fell inside his apartment room, alone and drunk. The room was dark except for a patch of red neon on the wall from a liquor sign flashing off and on outside the window. He had already reviewed the options for how he could end his life. He could use a gun.

"But if I missed, the pain and horror . . ."

He knew how to get to the top of the building. From there he could throw himself down onto the street, so he had started for the roof.

"But if I fell and survived . . ."

The thought of failing once more in life stopped him in the hallway and sent him back to his room, shaking.

He had bought some rat poison. He could wash it down with beer. It was all on the nightstand, ready to drink.

"I can do this. I can do this . . ."

His hands shook. He couldn't do it.

Now, sitting on his bed in a drunken stupor, Santos feared living one more day. He tried standing up. From the corner of his eye he saw another person in the room. The man was now moving toward him.

Santos spun around toward the dresser and threw out his arms. He saw the man staring him right in the eyes. It was a man he had seen before: it was his own face, staring back at him from the dresser mirror!

Santos looked at this sweaty, scruffy man with puffy cheeks. In his eyes he could see discouragement and the booze that had been mixed with years of self-pity and anger.

From the Jail to the Church

Santos had grown up poor on the outskirts of Los Angeles. For years he had scraped by on a string of odd jobs. Often the jobs had ended in layoffs. The layoffs had ended in fights. The fights landed Santos in jail. After several repeated offenses, he became a familiar, nagging sight to the judge who, eventually, ran out of patience. One day the judge looked at Santos and said, "You are trash. You are a disgrace to your race and to society. I want to lock you up and throw away the key."

After several months in jail, Santos believed the judge was ready to follow through on his wish. For breaking jail rules again, Santos was transported to another facility. As he rode in the van, fearful of facing the same judge, he remembered something he had heard one Sunday in church.

They were the words God had given to Joshua: "'Be strong and courageous. Do not be terrified; do not be discouraged, for the LORD your God will be with you wherever you go'" (Josh. 1:9).

Santos did not carry a Bible. He didn't read the Bible regularly, yet these words had stayed with him. They were his hope, his one reminder that, in prison, he had put his life in God's hands. He didn't necessarily expect anyone to believe him, least of all the one judge who seemed to have no mercy, the judge he now faced again. The magistrate looked down at Santos and said, "What would you do if I let you out?"

Santos peered up and said, "I am reformed, Your Honor."

He was not ready for the verdict.

"I'm going to trust you and release you," replied the judge.

Santos stood in shock. He was being set free on Easter Sunday.

He rode the elevator down to the main exit, and as Santos walked through the door that led out onto the street he prayed, "Lord, where is Your church?" Seconds after he stepped out into the sunlight, he saw the pastor and a deacon from the church he had attended months earlier. This was the church where Santos had first heard the words of Joshua.

For a while he got back on his feet. He stayed out of jail and returned to Mexico. Then, in a slow, self-destructive downward spiral, he forgot the grace of Easter Sunday. He forgot what faith looked like, acquired a taste for cheap beer, and began a daily devotion to booze.

Weeks of drinking had now brought him to the edge of his bed where he sat crying into his hands. Now, just a scrap of faith remained. "When I was younger I learned You were the Savior of the world. Jesus Christ, if You are true, if You really are God, then save me. Please, save me from myself."

The next morning Santos did something he hadn't done in years. He walked into a church. That morning he learned that the God he prayed to years ago, the God who had been with Joshua, was the same God who loved him uncondi-tionally, who knew every scrape and wrong turn he had made, and who, nonetheless, forgave him completely. This was the God Santos found that morning when he opened the Bible and saw the words that were now both familiar and new: "For God so loved the world that he gave his one and only Son, that whoever believes in him shall not perish but have eternal life" (John 3:16).

From that morning on, something began to change inside Santos Galan. Something was gnawing at him, something that prayer and reading the Bible brought to the surface. When he saw people at work, or passersby on the street, Santos saw thousands of Mexicans who had never heard or read the story of Jesus because they didn't have access to a Bible. Because of the lack of Scriptures, they would likely never have access to the one book that revealed God's power.

Santos knew that God was calling him to take this book and its gospel that had given him a new reason to live to others throughout Mexico. "Lord," he prayed, "I will do anything possible to tell others about how they can find new life and new hope in Jesus Christ." Within weeks Santos was living this prayer.

He began serving with a group called "Air Mail from God," appropriately named since it dropped Gospels of John from a single-engine Piper Cub. Santos's passion, however, was to preach at outdoor gatherings and during intermissions of Christian films. Relying on his loud, booming voice, he made five, six, even seven gospel presentations a day without the use of a microphone. After weeks of harsh sun, after ignoring his friends' suggestions to rest his voice, doctors found small tumors on Santos's throat.

He would never preach regularly again. In the midst of his dejection he met Chester Schemper from the Bible League, a group that provided Bibles and Scripture portions to church leaders in countries, like Mexico, that were without God's Word.

"If you preach, you can reach a few people at a time," said Schemper. "But if you distribute Bibles, you can reach hundreds, perhaps thousands."

The reality, Santos found, was that most pastors weren't interested in encouraging their members to give New Testaments to neighbors. "We've never done it before," they said. "Why should we start now?" Santos returned to his office, dejected. He thought about towns like Morelos and Colima where the Bible was as rare as rain. He wondered if he, or the Word, could make any difference.

Something Wonderful for Nahum

A few months later, in the summer of 1969, Nahum Gutierrez, a sixteen-year-old student living in the town of Colima, 350 miles west of Mexico City, was beside himself. His girlfriend of two years was now unexpectedly pregnant. He had no work, no money, no place to live. If she would

just get an abortion, he thought, all his anxiety would go
away. Esther wanted the baby. He just wanted to run.

Things had been so hard for so long Nahum couldn't
recall a time he felt happy. His only memory of childhood
was a fight between his father and mother. His four-year-
old sister became so scared by the shouting that she ran
out the front door into the street. Seconds later she was hit
by a speeding motorcyclist and injured for life.

After his parents' divorce, Nahum, his mother, and eight
siblings lived a life on the run. The only time Nahum saw
his mother was when she cooked dinner or tucked him in
bed. Although she never went to church, she would pick
him up, hold him in her arms, and say, "Here, Lord. This
one, Nahum, is yours."

He had run away from home at age eleven and was now
back in Colima. He eventually decided to marry Esther,
after the baby came, but things just got worse. Nahum
began beating his wife, who was pregnant again. The new
baby suffered epileptic seizures. One night her breathing
stopped, and Nahum blew into the girl's tiny mouth until
her chest began to move. *Now, if only someone could only
revive me*, he thought.

Nahum tried to escape the frustrations of his marriage
by rushing off to work. There he found men attracted to the
mysterious, unknown questions of life. Some were into
yoga. Others were fascinated by the idea of mind control,
astrology, extraterrestrial, and the Bible.

Nahum noticed how they would read a passage and then
explain what they thought it meant. Mostly he listened.
Because he had never read the Bible he felt he had nothing
to say, but all that changed. By the third or fourth week
Nahum began reading the Bible in his spare moments. His
colleagues liked mixing the Bible with yoga and other philosophies, but to Nahum it didn't feel right.

This book was like none he'd found, the only book
that showed God was real in history, alive in Jesus, and

present now through the Holy Spirit. Nahum began reading the New Testament with the Book of Matthew and didn't stop until he finished Revelation. When friends at work combined their philosophies with the Bible, Nahum asked, "Why can't we let the Bible speak to us and accept what it says?"

"Why should the Bible be the only truth?" said the others, who believed the pillar of cloud the Lord used to guide the Jews was a UFO. Instead of arguing, Nahum prayed, "Lord, if I'm wrong, change me. If they are wrong, change them." The next week, as the group read Exodus, the leader said, "I think we should stop thinking the cloud is a spaceship. What if we just read the Bible and accept what it says."

Nahum knew God had answered his prayers because he had it in writing: "The LORD is faithful to all his promises and loving toward all he has made" (Ps. 145:13). He and Esther were no longer arguing. They were standing back, aware that something wonderful was happening, something bigger than themselves.

Witness at Gunpoint

In the nearby town of Morelos, Santos Galan had spent eight hours one day going house to house with the New Testaments he hadn't been able to give away to pastors in Mexico City. The woman in the doorway held this book she had never seen before. "I want you to have this," he said to her. "I want you to know the message, the God, the new life—"

Without warning, a man carrying a gun appeared behind the woman. He stepped through the doorway and stuck the end of the barrel in Santos's stomach. "Get out of here," he said.

"Why do you want to kill me?" Santos asked calmly. "Do you want to kill me just because I tell you that God loves you? Did you know that God loves you? That's why Jesus

Christ came into the world, to die for you so that you could live."

The man's face drew a blank. He couldn't take his eyes off Santos. He laid down his gun, saying, "I think you're right."

An hour later, after reading through the Spanish Bible Santos put in his hands, the man said, "I want you to come back and tell my family what you just told me." Santos obliged. Two weeks later, Santos shared the gospel message with the man's entire kin. After Santos visited the home three days later, all fifteen family members, including the man himself, prayed to receive Jesus Christ as their personal Lord and Savior.

Santos thought to himself, *If God can use the Bible to change the life of a single individual, can't He do the same to change an entire church or community?* Where would he ever find the pastors, the people, or the workers who shared his vision?

A New Calling . . .

While Santos wondered these things to himself, Nahum Gutierrez now faced a sweet dilemma. His coworkers were no longer interested in parapsychology and flying saucers. Instead, they wanted only to read the Bible. One by one they had started praying together. Now, all five men and their wives had given their lives to God.

They chatted about the gospel at work. They told their neighbors and friends what had happened to them. They couldn't keep their excitement inside. Naturally, almost without thinking, they began helping people in Colima who had little or no food or clothes. Once they started, they felt no reason to stop.

As the weeks passed, the small group of ten agreed they needed the power of the Holy Spirit to lead them. Even though many of their prayers were being answered, they remained small in number. Something seemed to be missing. Then one day, while riding a bus from the town of Zanora, Nahum saw some startling words in a pamphlet: "The harvest is plentiful but the workers are few. Ask the Lord of the harvest, therefore, to send out workers into his harvest field" (Matt. 9:37–38).

Nahum knew God was calling him to be one of those workers in the harvest field of Colima. The next week he quit his job and became a full-time pastor.

Santos Meets Nahum

Santos Galan had never been to Colima. For a city of eighty thousand, it had only two or three evangelical churches. Santos had heard about one and their pastor, Nahum Gutierrez. Word had it he was interested in sharing the Bible with his people. One visit confirmed the report.

In Nahum, Santos met a natural leader and communicator who knew Colima's people. He knew their spiritual, emotional, and financial poverty. He had visited shut-ins, counseled troubled married couples, and comforted suicidal teens. These were people who began to find lasting solutions to their problems in the Bible, but so many others either didn't have their own Bible or chose not to read it. That's why Nahum liked Santos's idea: By simply going house to house and working with the other local evangelical churches, Nahum's church members could place a New Testament in every home in Colima.

Several months later, through much prayer and planning, that's exactly what happened. Christians from several small congregations—families and single people, mothers and fathers, teenagers and young children—handed hundreds of people the first New Testament they had ever seen. Santos's vision was the kindling for a blaze of new faith that swept through Colima.

As Santos left Colima to serve churches in other cities and towns, Nahum's church welcomed shopowners and farm laborers, travel agents and teachers, students and the elderly. All had one question for Nahum: "If the Bible is true, if it really is God's Word, then how can it speak to me? How can the Book, how can God, make a difference in my life today?"

Within the question Nahum could hear their honest doubts: Can I trust the Book? Can I take God at His Word even if it doesn't all make sense to me? Nahum's response was simple and direct: "Keep reading. Even if you don't understand it all, keep reading. The Bible is spiritual nourishment, like food is to our bodies. A baby doesn't grab hold of his bottle and say, 'Mother, I won't drink this unless you tell me all of the content and what it will do to my body!' A baby just drinks. You and I are the same way. When we begin to read the Bible, it starts nourishing our spirits, even if we don't understand it. Even when we can't possibly know the whys and hows of His ways, God can still be speaking to us and living in us."

Nahum then shared a personal story to illustrate what he meant. One day a woman approached him at church and said, "I've been coming to this church for some time. I've watched you, and there's something you have that I want. The only thing is, I don't believe what you believe about Jesus."

"You're not the only one who's ever doubted God," said Nahum. Then he shared the story of a man who had brought his son, possessed with an evil spirit, to Jesus:

> When the spirit saw Jesus, it immediately threw the boy into a convulsion. He fell to the ground and rolled around, foaming at the mouth.
>
> Jesus asked the boy's father, "How long has he been like this?"
>
> "From childhood," he answered. "It has often thrown him into fire or water to kill him. But if you can do any-

thing, take pity on us and help us."

"'If you can?'" said Jesus. "Everything is possible for him who believes."

Immediately the boy's father exclaimed, "I do believe; help me overcome my unbelief!" (Mark 9:20–24).

Nahum looked at the woman beset with her own doubts and said, "You are like this man. Jesus can help you. His love for you is bigger than your questions about the Bible. Invite the Lord Jesus to come into your life. Trust Him, trust His Word—even if you don't understand."

That night the woman followed through on what she didn't fully understand. She prayed to receive Christ.

From the next day she was a changed person. She took Bible courses at the church. She couldn't spend enough time reading the Bible. A few months later, Nahum saw her and asked, "How are you feeling?"

"Remember I told you I didn't believe in Jesus?" she said. "Well, now He's a part of my life. Though I don't understand everything in the Bible, I read it every day. Only by knowing this Book have I come to know Christ. He's given me a new reason to live."

When friends asked her why she was in such a hurry to know the Bible, the woman said, "I don't know; I just feel it's something I must do."

Two days later friends rushed her to the hospital. Doctors said the internal bleeding caused by a ruptured large intestine could not be stopped. "We can do no more to help you," they said.

Three days later the woman died.

At her memorial service, her widowed husband told a large gathering, "The last six months Carmona spent with us were the best of her entire life. You all know the reason why. It's because she met the Lord. Every day she came to know Him, love Him, and trust Him because she never stopped reading the Word."

People who came to Nahum with questions about the Bible, those who heard him tell this story, usually remembered one thing he said: "Even though you may not always understand what you read, the Bible will speak powerfully and directly to what you need."

Though every person's response varied, Nahum found, time and again, that beneath all the immediate pain and stress of their daily lives, what all people—new Christians like Carmona, tired Christians, hurting Christians, and non-Christians—often needed most was a new beginning, a new reason for living.

This simple insight is one reason why so many in Nahum's church began to read the Bible on a regular basis. They read it with curiosity. They read it with renewed interest. They read it with the expectation that God was going to change them as individuals, and as a church.

This God did. Santos saw it happening whenever he returned to Colima with new Bibles. Each time Santos came back, the church had more members. It seemed like only a matter of time before they would outgrow the renovated movie theater where they met for Sunday worship.

Outreach to Orphans

In only a few years the church grew from five families to 400 people. Nahum envisioned five to ten thousand people every Sunday and, along with the church's leaders, asked architects to design a large, new sanctuary to hold at least two thousand. To Santos Nahum said, "It will be spacious and beautiful, and it will glorify God. Already we've raised several thousands of dollars."

God had another building in mind, however. In an old, two-story structure a few blocks away, a Catholic priest ran an orphanage for homeless and abused children of Colima. To Nahum's delight, a few members of his church were already working with these boys and girls who had no parents.

In these children Nahum saw himself. In their eyes he saw the young boy of the father he never knew. In their anxious manners, he felt the frightened teen who had become an unwilling father at sixteen. In their profanity and crying, he heard God calling him to reach out; so Nahum went before his congregation one Sunday morning and said what was on his heart.

"We've all seen the beautiful drawings of the proposed sanctuary. It is something we have all prayed about. It is something we have all looked forward to because we are a people who love God and who want to serve Him.

"But this morning," he continued, "I want you to think of how you came to know the Lord. You came to know Him because someone once gave you a book you had never seen. In that book, you met a God you didn't know. Through the written Word you came to know the living Word, Jesus, and He changed your life.

"The Bible says, 'We love because He first loved us' (1 John 4:19). Because God has loved you, what or who are you going to love in return? I believe we have a choice: We can give our resources to a building; or, we can give ourselves to people in our own community who need our help. We can give the love of Jesus to those who need it most, our children, the children of Colima."

The people listened. That day they talked, and prayed, and asked God to show them His desire. That morning the men and women in Nahum's church voted down their plans for a new sanctuary. That day they decided to love the most needy in their midst, the neglected, hurting children in their city. Over the next weeks and months, men and women who had received a Bible from a stranger on their doorstep went to the front door of an orphanage to give their love, time, and prayers to children.

Today, these are the boys and girls who live at Hogar de Amor Y Proteccion Al Nino, A.C.—Home of Love and Protection for Children. Every week, several miles from Nahum's church, off the main road, a van rolls up a dirt trail to a clearing of grass and huge trees. Inside are church members who come to read stories, tutor, and simply be with boys and girls who have no moms and dads of their own.

Even before the van rolls to a stop, the children run outside. None of them is more than three feet tall. Behind each child is a name. Behind each name is a story.

Jose and Veronica are brother and sister. Their father is in prison; their mother is working on the streets of Colima. He cannot visit. She chooses not to visit.

Angel is four. His father left home to live with another woman. When the mother couldn't control her son, she brought him here and disappeared.

Doatel and Estina came without warning. One day their father drove up, got out of the car, and said, "Here they are. I can't stand them anymore." Then he turned around and left.

There are twenty-one children in all. They range in ages from five to fifteen. Though some share the same last name of their birth mother and father, they are all related by neglect. In their new, safe surrounding, they are happy because for the first time in their lives they feel loved. For the first time, they wake up to hugs and breakfast.

For the first time in their lives they hear about Jesus, and they believe. One day, because of families in Nahum's church, these children will say good-bye to Carmen and Robert Sawyer, the live-in caretaker couple who have chosen to be Mom and Dad to all twenty-one children. Someday, when they are older, they will want to know just how and why they came to be adopted. Even when they are old enough to have children of their own, however, these orphan children still will not know the two people who influenced their destiny the most. They will never really know the evangelist named Santos Galan and the electrical worker named Nahum Gutierrez, who began to read a book they didn't totally understand and yet couldn't put down.

Through this Book, a frustrated preacher and an impatient teenaged father discovered a new reason to live. As a result, a church found how much they had to give.

Going Deeper in the Word

This is how individuals like Santos, like Nahum, like you and like me, are changed—through a God whose Book speaks powerfully and directly to what you need right now, even when you don't always understand what you read.

Rekindling your love for God's Word can start by opening up and reading the Bible right where you are, right now! As Nahum Gutierrez discovered, it doesn't matter how much or how little you understand about the Word. What counts is that you take the time, even if it's just a few minutes, and begin reading.

One immediate way to do that is to turn to page 133. In chapter 9, "Making the Word Your Own: Twenty-eight Days That Could Change Your Life," you can start reading Scripture with the same sense of curiosity and adventure that led Nahum to love the Lord.

By exploring the Word, you'll begin to see how the Bible speaks your language. This very discovery that Wayne and Betty Snell made over the course of forty years you can know yourself by turning the page.

CHAPTER TWO

Exploring the Word

How the Bible Can Speak Your Language

————∞————

Therefore, I urge you, brothers, in view of God's mercy, to offer your bodies as living sacrifices, holy and pleasing to God—this is your spiritual act of worship.

Romans 12:1

But his followers took him by night and lowered him in a basket through an opening in the wall.

Acts 9:25

Words can't explain it. You don't understand how it happens. All you know is that it's real and exhilarating, and you wish it would happen much more often. One moment you're looking at words on a page, and then something catches your attention. You notice a phrase, a truth you've never seen before. You read it again. And again. Then it hits you: *It's as if these words were written for me. God's Word is speaking to me right where I live.*

How long has it been since you said these words to yourself? How can the Bible's truth be real for you again?

The answer may be found in a group of people most of the world has never met. For hundreds of years, the Machiguenga Indians lived in the jungles of Peru, isolated from the rest of the world, with no written language, and no knowledge of Christianity. Then they discovered a God who had revealed Himself through a one-of-a-kind book, *the* Book, they never knew existed. Today, their hope for life, their love for family, and their new sense of confidence and purpose bear little resemblance to a once-desperate existence rooted in fear.

Kept Alive for a Purpose

Wayne and Betty Snell are two of only a handful of people in the world who can tell this amazing story. They are some of the first outsiders to ever live and work with the Machiguengas in southeast Peru. On a warm afternoon in 1952, this couple stepped off a float plane and walked into a sun-drenched, humid world where they were greeted by the stares of silent strangers. They could not have known that these skittish, suspicious people would one day be teaching *them* precious, life-changing truths from the Machiguenga New Testament that, at the time, did not even exist.

It was a miracle that Wayne Snell ever made it to Peru in the first place. He was grateful just to be alive. As a child he had lain in bed with double pneumonia and scarlet fever. He had seen the same diseases kill his neighbors. One afternoon the seven-year-old heard the doctor tell his parents, "I'm leaving. He won't live until morning." All that night and into morning, Wayne's father, who knew nothing about mouth-to-mouth resuscitation, kept his son alive one breath at a time. By morning the crisis had passed.

Fourteen years later, Wayne Snell discovered his life had been saved once before. As a twenty-one-year-old sailor in the U.S. Navy, he read a book whose Author knew him by name: "For God so loved [Wayne Snell] that He gave His one and only Son, that [Wayne Snell], believing in him shall not perish but have eternal life [John 3:16]."

In the weeks that followed, as he served on the *USS Colorado* during World War II, Wayne spent hours memorizing verses of Scripture. Conversations with other sailors stirred his curiosity about world missions, about which he knew next to nothing. He began writing letters to Cameron Townsend, a missionary in Guatemala. Townsend's life had been changed one day when he tried to sell a Spanish Bible to a Guatemalan peasant. The man looked at Townsend and said, "If your God is so great, why can't He speak our language?" The experience moved Townsend to start a fledgling ministry that later became Wycliffe Bible Translators. Townsend's letters caused Wayne to pray about and consider a possible future in missions. After the war ended, Wayne attended Moody Bible Institute in Chicago where he met Betty. Several years later, assured that God had called them both to the work of Bible translation, the newly-married couple joined Wycliffe, and were assigned to Peru.

Searching for the Right Words

The Machiguenga Indians were one of the first peoples in Peru to benefit from Townsend's vision and the Snells' conviction: Without the Bible in their own language, the Machiguengas would never come to know Jesus Christ. Someone had to go to them, learn their language, and transform the sounds of their everyday speech into written words that would bring *the* Word to life. What the Snells offered was what the Machiguengas had sought for decades.

"What they wanted most of all," recalled Wayne, "is what people everywhere seek—eternal life. The Machiguengas wanted someone who could be their link, their forever lifeline, to the One who had created them.

"Without the Bible, the Machiguengas relied on a central creation myth. They believed they had been created by Tasorintsi and that, originally, they had been immortal. But through the unfortunate choice of one man, they had begun to get sick and die. Meanwhile, Tasorintsi left them and was never heard from again.

"For a time there was hope. For a time there had been an umbilical cord connecting the earth to the sky, a cord that earthbound mortals could climb to reach the land of the people who never die. One day the cord was severed, and the sky floated off farther and farther into space. Though the Machiguengas tried hard, no one had ever found a way to get back and know their Creator."

Unbeknownst to the Machiguengas, that Someone *had* come. The challenge, for Wayne and Betty Snell, was finding the right words to tell the story that had already been written.

Clash of Cultures

"Translating the Bible into the Machiguenga language," said Betty, "meant communicating concepts and truths penned in the context of desert sands or urban areas, by men steeped in patterns of Jewish thought and religious background at the height of the Roman Empire. These concepts and truths then had to be transferred into the language and thought patterns of a jungle people who had absolutely no concept of the political or religious institutions of their own country, much less those of a far-off, long-ago Roman Empire and Jewish nation. Translating the Bible into the Machiguenga language meant finding words where no words existed for even the most concrete things such as deserts, wells, sheep, cities, marketplaces, and jails."

From the moment they arrived in Peru, Betty and Wayne had no trouble finding words to describe what they saw. "The Machiguengas' world was a huge, green forest," said Betty. "At night it became an orchestra that tuned up with the sounds of hundreds of cicadas and other nocturnal creatures. Out of this humid jungle walked a brown-skinned people whose faces were streaked with orange paint and whose sense of humor was often expressed at our own expense. The Machis were so curious they would walk into our house and literally camp out! They wanted to touch everything, skin, clothes, hair—and children! One night a Machiguenga woman picked up ten-month-old Ron and tried to nurse him."

The flip side of the Machiguengas' curiosity was much less friendly. The truth was, they didn't want the Snells around. They feared one another, living in scattered, extended-family clusters throughout a vast area of dense rain forest. Their only connecting links were the swift flowing rivers that served as a kind of one-stop market, bathtub, and laundromat.

By day the Machiguengas fished, hunted, cultivated small garden plots, and spun the necessities of daily life out of what the jungle provided. At night they barricaded themselves inside leaf-roofed homes to keep out dangers, seen and unseen. Punctuated by the beat of hand-carved drums and raucous laughter, their all-night, drunken orgies were their only escape from a life of isolation.

"The Machiguengas had no communities, no villages, and no love, not even for their fellow Machiguengas," wrote former Wycliffe President George Cowan. "If a neighbor was drowning in a raging stream, they let him drown. If he slipped on the trail, they let him slip. Every man fended for himself." [1]

Dying of Fear

To Betty and Wayne, translating the New Testament couldn't come soon enough. Every day the Machiguengas lived without the Scriptures, they lived in fear of a dark,

---

1. George Cowan, "A People of the Book," *In Other Words* (April/May 1984).

supernatural reality that could take their lives at any time. Betty Snell saw it with her own eyes:

"We were moving to a new community one day. The children and I went by plane, and Wayne set out in a dugout canoe with a Machiguenga language helper and another Machiguenga friend. In a surge of swift water the canoe slammed into a tree, and the language helper drowned. This is when tribal belief took over.

"The Machis believed that during the next five days the dead man was still around, gathering discarded possessions and trying to take family members with him to his next life. Therefore, it was important not to go anywhere alone for fear of being taken, but one person ignored the warnings. He went into the woods with an ax to chop down a bee hive—and promptly cleaved his foot.

"Just after this man died of tetanus, his brother fell prey to the Machiguenga belief that the dead person's spirit goes into an animal. In this case it was a stork that had landed on the porch of the injured man. When his brother shot the stork, he noticed that the placement of the wounds on the bird looked disturbingly similar to the spots that had been rubbed raw on the victim's body.

"The now-fearful brother believed the dead language helper had taken one more person. After touching his dead brother's body he feared for his own life and that of his pregnant wife. When his wife delivered her baby, it was stillborn.

"Because his wife was now a 'link' in this chain reaction of death, she knew she wasn't supposed to talk to any other woman who had not lost a child; but she ignored tradition. She lifted up the blanket of another woman's sick child to take a peek, and within a few days the child died."

The Machiguengas were literally dying in the face of their greatest fears. "What they feared and expected really happened, not because they wanted it to but because something more powerful than them was at work," said

Betty. How could God's Word, which did not yet exist in their language, be greater than daily reminders of death?

Breaking Down Fear

The only ways the Machiguengas could receive the gospel, medical help, or schooling were: either they would choose to leave their scattered clusters and come together in larger groups, or their own people would reach out to them. Remarkably, a little bit of both brought them together for the first time in their history.

Education and community development were the magnets that drew the Machiguengas out of the jungle and toward one another. As people were trained as teachers, they invited others to form tiny communities. With Wayne's help, the Machiguengas learned how to help themselves. They learned how to grow crops that could then be sold for money to buy needed medicine.

Each time they learned something new, such as how to build furniture or how to power a new fishing boat with a small gasoline engine, the Machiguengas' clenched fist of fear relaxed into an open hand of trust. They realized this white-skinned couple wanted to give them things they never had, like self-sufficiency—and words. To appreciate their discovery of the latter, put yourself in the Machiguengas' place.

Imagine never having seen your spoken language in print. Then imagine the sounds of your mouth being captured on paper. Slowly, you come to discover your language has an alphabet of twenty-two letters. With these characters you're able to form something called "words" that allow you to look at thoughts and truths you never knew existed.

As you begin to learn to read your new language, captured on leaves of paper, you begin to learn that Tasorintsi, the One you were told about for years, knows your words, knows your language, and knows what you need. In fact, you learn a book exists that reveals who Tasorintsi really is, how God created the world, nature, and human beings. As this book becomes translated, word by word, line by line, you gradually come to see that it's everything the American translator couple said it was, a one-of-a-kind revelation. By knowing this book you come to know the One you've worshiped and prayed to all these years.

Open to the Word

Making this book known became a daily discipline of love. For months the Snells translated oral sounds to phonetic script, "cooking them down" first into written symbols, then into a working alphabet, and finally into words. After hours of searching and experimenting, Betty and Wayne finally settled on the words that best captured the life and meaning of Scripture in the Machiguengas' own language. Then, out loud, the Snells read and reread passages with the Machiguengas, hoping they would understand and believe. As they did all this, the Snells constantly asked themselves, "How do we know God's Word is getting through? Is the Word speaking to them in a way they understand?"

Through daily examples of changed lives, this is what Betty and Wayne Snell came to admit: What allowed the Machiguengas to know the God who spoke their language was that they came to Scripture as strangers to the truth. Their lack of knowledge wasn't a barrier, but rather an open gate through which the Holy Spirit flowed.

Translation: Because the Machiguengas knew so little, they were ready to learn so much. Uncluttered by theological biases, doubts, or a Bible familiarity that breeds indifference, they came to Scripture curious, continually open to what they might find. They made the startling connection that the one true God had visited earth as Jesus Christ, fulfilling a promise of eternal life their long-held myth had denied them for generations.

A God She Could Trust

Once they could read and understand the words of the One they had longed to know, the Scriptures hit like lightning. Like a young Helen Keller learning to say the word water as it ran over her hands, the Machiguengas realized *the* special Book didn't just talk about a promised eternal life, it offered a new way to live, *because in the words was life itself.* As a woman named Isolina discovered, knowing *the* Book meant the difference between life and death.

The Snells had known Isolina as a child. They were there for her when her mother committed suicide. As Isolina grew up, she came to love the book Betty and Wayne shared with her. When Isolina became desperately ill with what later was diagnosed as an elongated appendix, the women in her village wanted her to take some special herbs touted for their supernatural curative powers, but Isolina refused.

"I will not eat the herbs," she said. "I will trust God."

The women bristled. "Well then, let God feed you too." For the next several days they refused to lift a hand to help supply the food that Isolina, her partially handicapped husband, and children needed to live. Depending on the Word meant she had nothing to fall back on, nowhere to turn for help—no doctor, no hospital, no place to buy food, and no group of caring Christians among her own people. Isolina had nothing to count on but the words that promised life and hope. Faithful to His written promise, the God she knew as Tasorintsi led her to a skilled surgeon and complete recovery.

Nothing Hidden from God

Sometimes the new Scriptures were so clear to the Machiguengas that Betty herself stood back in amazement. One day a group of Machiguengas came to Betty with

Jesus' familiar words about hiding a lamp. This is how the Machiguenga translation sounded in English:

> "When a kerosene wick lamp is lit, it isn't covered up with a cooking pot. And it's not placed under a sleeping platform. It's put on top of the platform so that everyone who's sitting there will be in the light. In that same way, everything that is hidden now will be caused to be revealed later on, and whatever isn't known will be known because nothing will be hidden again. And that's why you need to really listen as I tell you that he who hears the Word of God, God will teach him and he will hear and learn even more. But the one that doesn't want to hear and understand it will keep on forgetting everything that he heard in vain, because he doesn't really know it." (Luke 8:16–18)

To Betty the meaning was obvious: Christians are supposed to let their lights shine; but a Machiguenga woman, reading it for the first time, heard something different. In fact the message was so obvious to her she told her friends. Soon, numerous Machiguenga women began arriving on the Snells' front porch. Each woman had taken Jesus' words to heart. What they couldn't stop talking about had nothing to do with shining a light.

"One by one," said Betty, "they all said, 'I don't want anything hidden in my life. If there's anything hidden in my life, I want to tell it to you now, because I don't want it to appear later on.'

"These women who had never seen the Bible showed me something new, something I had never seen. Reading and knowing the Bible wasn't about grabbing hold of 'the right' translation and shining a light, it was about living differently in light of God's truth.

"One young, concerned woman said to me, 'Remember when I was sick and I lived with you at your house? I took some of your extra underwear. I don't want that to be hidden and come out later on.'"

Women who heard about the "hidden" meaning from friends came to Betty with a look of conviction in their eyes. Each woman said she wanted to be forgiven for the things she had kept hidden from God. Betty assured them of God's promise: "If we confess our sins, he is faithful and just and will forgive us our sins and purify us from all unrighteousness" (1 John 1:9).

"For years," said Wayne, "we didn't really know what impact our translation was having until we discovered the Machiguenga word for 'believe.' It also means 'obey.' If I explained a word, a phrase, or a passage and a person said, 'I hear it,' what he or she really meant was, 'I will do it.' For them, 'believing' and 'doing' were one and the same."

When Faith Translates to Action

"God was now using the Machiguengas to speak our language," said Wayne. "Take the classic passage of Romans: 'Therefore, I urge you, brothers, in view of God's mercy, to offer your bodies as living sacrifices, holy and pleasing to God—this is your spiritual act of worship' (Rom. 12:1).

"In Machiguenga, there's no word for 'body,' and no word for 'sacrifice.' Therefore it seemed the best way to capture the meaning in Machiguenga was to say: 'Now my fellow believers, since you have seen how God has had mercy and pity on you, I really want to tell you that it is good for you to tell God, "Now Father God, I want you to really own me in order that I will dedicate myself to you alone, to obey You. Whatever you tell me to do, I'll do it."'"

At first glance, it might seem that the Machiguenga language didn't have precise words to match the text. However, as Wayne and Betty realized, they were the right words the Machiguengas needed to believe. To them Paul's message of "living sacrifices" became nothing less than a clear call to action: "That's it Lord, I'll do it. I've got to do it."

Ready to Die, Ready to Live

To Arturo, a Machiguenga former slave boy, there was no separating what he read from how he lived. As a young man, he had made a solid profession of faith in Christ, and he later trained as a bilingual teacher to serve his people. One day, Wayne met with the Machiguenga teachers to talk about reaching another group of their tribe who, isolated by mountains and miles of thick forest, was not aware that the Words of Tasorintsi existed.

Wayne asked, "Which of you will volunteer to go and start a school among these people?" Only Arturo spoke up.

"I'm ready to go," he said. "Those are my people. God has called me to give them the gospel." Arturo was in no physical shape to make the grueling journey. Sick with consumption, he walked for four days over rugged mountains to gather the people together.

In five months, Arturo reproduced the strategy Betty and Wayne had used in his village. First, he started a school. Then, by teaching this other isolated group of Machiguengas their own written language, he taught them how to read the Bible.

Initially, seventy-seven people responded to Arturo's invitation to form a new village around the new school he had started. Weeks later, ninety-seven Machiguengas, twenty more than logically seemed possible, received Christ! To the Snells there was only one explanation: Those who heard and believed the gospel went back to their former homes and told others about this new revelation of God. Once again "believing" meant "doing" for the Machiguengas, who heard God speaking their language.

This language—the Words of Tasorintsi, the Word of God—transformed Machiguenga villages one life at a time.

Take Mariano. He had been born four hundred miles away from civilization in a leaf-roofed jungle home and had grown up a slave. By the time he was ten his two desires in life were to be one of the best workers in his community and to share the gospel of Jesus Christ with everyone who would listen.

One of those who heard Mariano share the story was a man named Angel. As Angel believed God, he told the story to his father, Marino, who also received the new Word the Snells had made known. Soon after he read that Jesus had spent forty days in the desert, Marino, the father, asked himself, "Why shouldn't I do that?" Barefoot and alone, he walked into the jungle to fast and pray. Four days later, he emerged with a message for his people: "When the day grows dark, when the sun dies and night descends, the vermin come out. Creatures that live in the dark love the dark, need the dark, but shine your flashlight and they turn back. They can't stand the light. Our brightness, our light for tonight and forever, is the Word of God."

As the New Testament became translated into their own language, the Machiguengas had what they had been missing all their lives, a light that was able to push back the darkness of unknowing so they could see Tasorintsi, their God. Holding on to this light of truth, hope, and life, the Machiguengas, who had always lived alone in clusters, came out of the dark corners of the forest and turned from a life of isolation into peaceful, cooperative communities.

Once they were able to read and write, the Machiguengas never looked back. A new, written language gave them words that allowed them to communicate and teach skills as promoters, storekeepers, carpenters, mechanics, and seamstresses. The first Machiguenga children to read and write their own language could understand the Book of Tasorintsi. Generations of fear and hopelessness were broken. No longer would they have to succumb to their parents' fatalistic outlook of "tomorrow we die."

Forty years after their arrival in Peru, Betty and Wayne Snell experienced the ultimate proof that God's Word speaks directly and powerfully in one's own language. This is how the people who once had no written language—no Bible—taught the Snells a truth about God's love they never knew.

Freedom from Fear

In 1992, Betty and Wayne returned to help with needed revisions of the Machiguenga New Testament. Forty years after the Snells' arrival, the villagers bore little resemblance to the fearful, scattered people who had once shown the Snells contempt. Things that had once seemed impossible were now commonplace. Fathers and sons walked together. People from different families actually got along with one other. People who had always lived apart now came together to trade, visit, and worship. The biggest surprise to Betty and Wayne was what happened in the actual Bible-revision sessions.

The Snells had arrived for the Bible-revision work while the Peruvian government was fighting a guerrilla war. While the neighboring countryside sizzled with gunfire, the Machiguengas brought the Snells to a refuge tucked away from the fighting. For the next four months, eight hours a day, for five, sometimes six, days a week, the Snells and four Machiguenga church leaders clarified the Book that had touched and transformed an entire culture.

One day they were studying the story of how Jewish leaders threatened to kill Paul. This was the pivotal verse: "But his followers took him by night and lowered him in a basket through an opening in the wall" (Acts 9:25). The translation team approached the passage like any other. Aware that the meaning could hinge on a single word, they had to make sure the verb was correct.

Betty asked, "What about the word that means 'causes him to flee'? In Paul's case, the people who let him down were not the ones from whom he was fleeing."

One of the Machiguengas looked up and said, "That's exactly right." He thought of the nearby fighting and said,

"We are like Paul's friends in the passage; what they did out of friendship is just what we're going to do for you if the opposition forces come. The only difference is that your escape to safety would come in the jungle instead of in a basket."

In this single pledge of sacrifice, forty years of living, and giving, and translating the Scriptures hit home. Betty and Wayne Snell looked around the table and saw people who were ready to risk their own lives to ensure the Snell's safety.

Love That Won't Let You Go

The Snells knew something had changed. The people who had once touched their skin out of curiosity had now been touched by the Book and its message of love. With words that translated into action, the Machiguengas showed that the best way to understand the Bible was to live it.

The Snells learned that two Machiguenga words are used for "love." The first love describes someone you want to marry; it's used only before you marry. This is love "to want" or "to like." The Machiguengas didn't know that this kind of love defined so many people in American culture longing for love that's still "out there somewhere."

The Machiguengas had their own meaning of love that English couldn't define. As they explained to Betty and Wayne, this second kind of love isn't a longing for something you don't have; it's something that's real, permanent, and present. This second kind of love means "to be attached, to not want to be separated, to not want to let go."

As soon as the Machiguengas said these words, Betty told the translation team, "This love that you just described is what really describes God's love. His love is a love that 'won't let you go.'"

In this "Ah ha!" moment, Betty Snell heard God speak her language. Yet, she still had a question.

"Your definition of love is so good, so right, so consistent with God's love. Yet how can this 'present, here-and-now' love, this love that means 'to be attached, to not be separated,' apply to 'loving all believers' when they are absent? How can this love—God's love—be real to someone who's far away, who's actually separated from you?"

The Machiguengas smiled. Betty waited for their answer, not realizing she had just described how she and Wayne had lived the past eight years, separated from their Peruvian friends.

One of the Machiguengas then spoke. "The reason we could love you with God's love," he said, "is that, in a spiritual sense, we weren't separated from you at all, because while you were gone, we loved you in prayer. While we didn't see you, even though we were separated from you, we prayed for you; that's the definition of God's love. When you pray for someone you're loving that person, you're united with that person, and you're doing what the Bible says, 'loving all believers.'"

In that moment, in a very real way, Betty and Wayne Snell heard the Word of God for the first time.

What allowed the Snells to rekindle their understanding, their appreciation, and their love for God's Word is that they approached the Scriptures as students. Like the Machiguengas before them, what they didn't know became an open gate through which the Holy Spirit flowed to teach and guide.

For Wayne and Betty Snell, just like for anyone renewed by the Word, that "Ah ha!" moment of discovery is a two-sided wonder. We see the Truth for the first time and want to see it again.

This is the delight of knowing, and the desire of always wanting to know more. This is when the light pushes back the darkness, revealing a Lord you've never seen or heard, a Word worth exploring, and a God who speaks your own language.

Going Deeper in the Word

Imagine reading the Bible with the attitude that says, "Lord, I come to Your Word as a student. Show me what I don't yet know about You." This is the very attitude that revolutionized the Machiguenga culture and drew Betty and Wayne Snell into a new lifelong love of God's Word.

By turning to page 144, you can begin reading Scripture with a new openness to learn. In chapter 9, you can explore Scripture using several practical study insights that brought the Word to life for the Machiguengas.

By exploring the Word you'll begin to see words and phrases you never noticed before, just like a couple from the city of Minsk, Belarus, whose love for God and the Bible was ignited by simply noticing some of the smallest, ignored details in Scripture. Their story has never been told in print until now.

CHAPTER THREE

Examining the Word

How the Bible Can Renew Your Mind

———— ∞ ————

The angel said to the women, "Do not be afraid, for I
know that you are looking for Jesus, who was crucified. He
is not here; he has risen, just as he said. Come and see the
place where he lay. Then go quickly and tell his disciples:
'He has risen from the dead and is going ahead of you into
Galilee. There you will see him.' Now I have told you."

So the women hurried away from the tomb, afraid yet
filled with joy, and ran to tell his disciples.

Matthew 28:5-8

Eugene Monakoff and Helene Vorobyova live in Minsk, a
city of 1.5 million people in the former Soviet republic of
Belarus. At first glance they seem no different from other
young married couples in the area. They don't own a car.
Both work to earn enough money for food, rent, clothes—
and books. Their living room is filled with them. One book
in particular sits on their small kitchen table. For years,
Eugene and Helene had never taken the Bible seriously.
Today, they read it regularly at meals, during times of
prayer, or with longtime friends who don't know what to
make of them.

Something happened. Somewhere along the line for
Eugene and Helene, the Bible went from being a

conversation piece to a source of truth and daily inspiration. At some point, they will tell you, the Bible began to stir their curiosity and raise questions they had been keeping inside for years. As their thinking changed, so did their lives.

By simply reading, and reflecting, and asking some honest, straightforward questions—by examining the Word—Eugene and Helene experienced true renewal, that moment when understanding and faith come together. In their new learning that led to new faith, they discovered Christ alive in the Word, and alive in each other.

One Boy's Deepest Longing . . .

Eugene Monakoff grew up as an only child in Kaunas, Lithuania. Like many kids whose parents were pulled apart by social, economic, and personal pressures, he never saw his father. To survive, Eugene's mother worked as a janitor. Often, while she cleaned, Eugene would help swab toilets and mop floors. She wanted him to work hard. She wanted him to know and believe and live the Communist way of life. If he did these things, she believed, Eugene would grow up to be a success.

Their life was rough. Their days were filled with regular housing shortages, health problems, and constant poverty. "At the time I never realized how poor we really were," said Eugene. "I just knew there were some things I couldn't have. I couldn't ask for a banana. I couldn't ask for a piece of cake. I would never think of asking my mother for a bike, better shoes, or a new T-shirt. Instead I learned to be content with what I had."

What Eugene did have was books. Before he was old enough to sit up, his mother put a book in his hands. At first she gave him children's stories, then history texts and world classics, including Russian novels by Dostoyevsky and Tolstoy. "All the walls in our apartment, from ceiling to floor, were lined with bookshelves. I longed to know more and to read more."

Eugene's curiosity eventually led him to college. In 1992 he graduated from a highly respected university, then taught English and French to privileged high school students. That same year he married. While Helene worked in a city eight hundred miles away, Eugene attended the Language Institute in Minsk. Without thinking seriously how he could put his valuable talents to work, he began mastering English. Eugene lived (and drank) the moment. Days were reserved for studying, nights for dancing. The pattern remained unbroken until one fateful evening.

When Opportunity Knocked

Eugene was relaxing in his twelfth-floor dormitory room when he heard a knock at the door. A man walked in, a Russian named Miraslov Sokolov. He explained to Eugene that out of all the dormitories on campus he had chosen this one. Out of all the floors he had come to the twelfth. Instead of going down the left hall, he had gone right. "Of all the doors to knock on," he said, "I chose yours."

"What do you want?" Eugene asked.

"I'm looking for interpreters," said Sokolov. "With the end of the Cold War and the Soviet Union, with the doors now open to new visitors, a group of American Christians is headed here in a few days. They're coming to bring their message to school children. Would you be interested in being one of their interpreters?"

Eugene sat up. He had just one question: "How much would you pay me?"

"Five hundred rubles a month," said Sokolov. To a struggling graduate student who was glad to own a pair of shoes, five hundred rubles was a small fortune. Whether the people were Christians or not didn't really matter.

"I need two interpreters to fly to Moscow tomorrow," said Sokolov. "Are you interested?"

It took Eugene less than twenty minutes to pack his travel bag. That night he looked over his assignment. He would accompany a party of twenty men and women. They would go to an elementary school where the Americans would talk to the children about their belief in God and the importance of the Bible.

Nothing Eugene had seen on television about the U.S., not even the little he knew about the Bible, could have prepared him for what happened when the first group of American Christians arrived in Moscow. The school's principal met Eugene and the other interpreter in front of the building. There were polite handshakes and nervous smiles. Then the principal led them into a classroom where thirty sets of eyes stared at them.

It was the first time these Russian children had ever seen Americans. They had heard words like "Atlantic Ocean," "United States," and "New York City." Few, including Eugene, were familiar with the words of the group's leader. For the first time in his life, a twenty-four-year-old language student from Minsk, a person raised on atheism, began to say words he had never thought about, much less believed:

"There is a God who created you, who knows you and loves you, and who lives today."

"There is a person named Jesus, God in human form, who once lived on earth, and who is alive today."

"There is a book that tells how you can know this Jesus and explains why you were born, why you're here on this earth, and where you're going. This book is yours to read, to learn, and to know."

Something Impossible to Ignore

As Eugene interpreted the words of the American leader he thought about the Bible, that it was not an easy book to come by in his country. What the group leader was saying in English about knowing God—finding peace and purpose in life—were words he had never heard spoken in his native Russian until now. As he spoke, all the children listened. As he talked about God, he realized he was eavesdropping on himself, listening in on a story he didn't quite believe but a story he also couldn't quite ignore.

After the group leader completed his remarks, the visitors passed out copies of the book to each of the school children. Then Eugene saw one of the strangest things he had ever witnessed: the American Christians began to hug the children. Not only had they taken time off from work and paid their own way to come to his country, not only were they giving away books, but also they were hugging the children.

They did something else that Eugene couldn't believe: some of the Americans opened up their wallets and purses and showed pictures of husbands, wives, and children. Eugene couldn't resist looking. He saw something good in these pictures, something attractive, something he couldn't ignore.

That night, after the Americans retired to hotel rooms, Eugene and the other three interpreters compared notes. They shook their heads and laughed about the American Christians. All four agreed, "First of all, they're crazy. Second of all, they're holy. Third of all, they're crazy."

Crazy enough that later the first night Eugene began reading the Bible stories he had interpreted earlier in the day. *Maybe there is something in this book,* he thought. When he returned home from his first "missionary" journey several days later, he said nothing to Helene. She could tell, however, this wasn't the same man she had married. Staying up late drinking and dancing did not appeal to him now.

For weeks Helene had tried to secure airline tickets to see her parents. After the tickets arrived, Helene said, "I can't believe how lucky I am."

"You're not lucky," Eugene replied calmly. "That's God helping you."

"What did these people do to you?" Helene asked. All her life she had been taught there was no God and that Communism would take care of everything. But now, those long-held promises, like the country itself, were crumbling all around her.

God of the Impossible

"What do you really believe about Christianity?" Helene asked Eugene. "Do you really believe that God exists, that He lived, that Jesus walked? Do you really believe it?"

"Yes," he said.

"I don't believe there is a God," she replied.

Two things happened to change Helene's view. The next week Eugene phoned her to say a new interpreter position with visiting Christian groups had just opened up. Could she resign her teaching job in five days and join him? In the Communist system, this was asking the impossible. Knowing she needed a miracle, Helene asked to resign. Without hesitation her boss said yes, no strings attached.

A second "impossible" happened when Helene told one of the American Christians about having ongoing nightmares. The American woman asked her, "Do you pray?"

"No," said Helene.

"Try praying," said the woman. "Pray a very short prayer: 'Dear Jesus, help me. Your blood was shed for me. I believe in You. Amen.'" From that night on, the nightmares ceased.

Helene continued to look at Christianity and thought, *I'll never believe in this God, this Jesus.* "Never" lasted a little more than three weeks. In a total reversal of mind and heart, she embraced Jesus as Lord and Savior. What made the difference, what brought her out of a life of doubt and cynicism into a new freedom of loving herself and others, and what made God come alive was the Bible.

For years it had been a dead book to her, but that changed. As she and Eugene began to read the Bible, they gained a few revealing approaches that helped them learn and apply virtually any Bible passage they read. The results were nothing short of revolutionary.

"To many people in Belarus where we live, and the other former countries in the Soviet Union, the Bible had no life," said Helene. "The Bible wasn't like modern fiction, filled with lots of action. It wasn't like an exciting film with a dramatic, fast-moving story line. Instead, at first, the Bible seemed to be dry, static, and quite boring."

Huge Details . . .

That began to change for Eugene and Helene when a visiting American pastor became the catalyst for three practical discoveries that helped them see how much they were missing in the Scriptures, Said the pastor, "If you're plunging into the Bible for the first time, you're like the person who's familiar with Scripture yet desires the words to be new. That newness isn't found so much in the 'big picture' but in the details many tend to overlook.

"Take the morning of the Resurrection, for instance," the pastor said to Eugene and Helene. "Here's what we know from Matthew's Gospel:" 'After the Sabbath, at dawn on the first day of the week, Mary Magdalene and the other Mary went to look at the tomb. There was a violent earthquake, for an angel of the Lord came down from heaven and, going to the tomb, rolled back the stone and sat on it. His appearance was like lightning, and his clothes were white as snow. The guards were so afraid of him that they shook and became like dead men' [Matt. 28:1–4]."

The pastor said to Eugene and Helen, "Many Christians who've read the Resurrection story many times already know the ending. The tendency is to focus on the obvious: the stone that's been rolled away from the tomb—but there's more to the story. The reality, the life of the Resurrection, is in the next few lines: 'The angel said to the women, "Do not be afraid, for I know that you are looking for Jesus, who was crucified. He is not here; he has risen, just as he said. Come and see the place where he lay. Then go quickly and tell his disciples: 'He has risen from the dead and is going ahead of you into Galilee. There you will see him.' Now I have told you." So the women hurried away from the tomb, afraid yet filled with joy, and ran to tell his disciples' (Matt. 28:5–8).

"'Afraid, yet filled with joy.' A huge stone may reveal the empty tomb," continued the pastor, "but it's the feelings of two women that reveal the awesome reality of the resurrected Christ and engage our minds in the story. Think of it. 'Afraid, yet filled with joy' is how you or I would feel inside if we were running down the road on that first Easter."

Suddenly Scripture is not so boring. It's real; it's urgent; it's alive.

"Take Luke's account: 'When they came back from the tomb, they told all these things to the Eleven and to all the others. It was Mary Magdalene, Joanna, Mary the mother of James, and the others with them who told this to the apostles. But they did not believe the women, because their words seemed to them like nonsense. Peter, however, got up and ran to the tomb. Bending over, he saw the strips of linen lying by themselves, and he went away, wondering to himself what had happened' [Luke 24:9–12].

"'Peter, however, got up and ran to the tomb.' This small sentence tends to get lost in the shadow of the stone that's been moved away from the tomb. Yet, the only one who did not consider the angel's revelation to the women to be nonsense was Peter. He had to find out what happened to Jesus. What news of the Resurrection did for Peter, the Good News of the Bible should do for us, and that leads us to look for Jesus."

Practical insight number one: Familiar Bible passages come alive as you discover the take-it-for-granted details that can unlock the feelings, motivations, and faith of characters in whom we see ourselves.

The pastor then shared a second suggestion for examining Scripture that logically piggybacked on the "revealing details" of the first insight. It was actually Eugene who made the discovery. In a well-known passage, Eugene found the kind of fresh, new meaning people want when they read the Bible, people who are tempted to say, "I know what this story is about. I've read it before." *This* is the story Eugene and Helene read for the first time:

> One day as he was teaching, Pharisees and teachers of the law, who had come from every village of Galilee and from Judea and Jerusalem, were sitting there. And the power of the Lord was present for him to heal the sick. Some men came carrying a paralytic on a mat and tried to take him into the house to lay him before Jesus. When they could not find a way to do this because of the crowd, they went up on the roof and lowered him on his mat through the tiles into the middle of the crowd, right in front of Jesus.
>
> When Jesus saw their faith, he said, "Friend, your sins are forgiven."
>
> The Pharisees and the teachers of the law began thinking to themselves, "Who is this fellow who speaks blasphemy? Who can forgive sins but God alone?"
>
> Jesus knew what they were thinking and asked, "Why are you thinking these things in your hearts? Which is easier: to say, 'Your sins are forgiven,' or to say, 'Get up

and walk'? But that you may know that the Son of Man has authority on earth to forgive sins. . . ." He said to the paralyzed man, "I tell you, get up, take your mat and go home." Immediately he stood up in front of them, took what he had been lying on and went home praising God. Everyone was amazed and gave praise to God. They were filled with awe and said, "We have seen remarkable things today." (Luke 5:17–26)

Suddenly, for Eugene and Helene, this biblical account they had read before was new. Eugene couldn't hide his excitement. He turned to the pastor and said, "This is remarkable. By seeing a few revealing details—the removed tiles up above, and the mat lowered down through the hole in the roof—this story became real. It's as if we were experiencing the moment *in the living room with Jesus.*

Helene said, "This wasn't some anonymous person's home, it was *our* home. Someone was climbing up on our roof, tearing off tiles, and making a mess of the living room. When I began to actually participate in the story, I couldn't help but think, *What are these people doing lowering a man through a hole into our home?*

"Then it became clear to me: the only person who could help this paralyzed man was Jesus. In the Word, Jesus was right in our midst. If it were my home, I would have been angry about our furniture and rugs being torn up. Yet the only thing that impressed Jesus was the faith of people who would do anything so that their friend would be healed."

Eugene took Helene's observation and the power of Scripture's revealing details and combined them into another practical insight:

Practical insight number two: *The overlooked details of Scripture not only help make the Scripture new for us,* *they also draw us into the Scripture itself by showing us what we know and don't know about the characters.*

Eugene, the one who had been so far away from Scripture, now made a wonderful, surprising connection that showed God had already been renewing his mind through the Word.

Faceless People Become Real

"Let me ask you a question," he said to the pastor. "What makes good literature? Take some of the great authors—Dickens, Goethe, or Tolstoy. The characters in their stories are alive. In some cases they're more alive than you or me because the author uses descriptions, mood, setting, and dialogue. Often, however, in the Bible, we don't find this kind of vividness. We don't have large, descriptive backgrounds. Instead, we get only little snippets of information. Instead of an in-depth description of Andrew, all we read is, 'Andrew.' Instead of a lot of background of Matthew, we simply get, 'Matthew, tax collector.'"

Now it was the visiting American pastor who was sitting up.

"Though the Bible is filled with wonderful characters, it seems to me we may not appreciate them right away," said Eugene. "We need to know how to look for the clues that will help us notice who these people really are and what they may be telling us about how to live.

"Remember the rough welcome Paul and Barnabas received when they came to Antioch? 'But the Jews incited the God-fearing women of high-standing and the leading men of the city. They stirred up persecution against Paul and Barnabas, and expelled them from their region' (Acts 13:50).

"As a description, it's not all that much," said Eugene. "You can read it as fact, or you can go one step further.

When we came to this passage with the schoolchildren I asked them, 'Can you imagine an angry crowd of women?' Some shut their eyes and thought hard. 'Can you see what Paul and Barnabas faced?' I asked. 'Can you see two helpless men being chased down the street by a pack of women and men?'

"First the kids just smiled, then they broke out laughing. They could actually see what Luke was talking about. Then I had them draw what they had just 'seen' in the passage. I looked down at one boy's piece of paper, and I saw two of the church's first great leaders, Paul and Barnabas, hiding in the bushes. That boy, that class, will remember this passage forever because the characters became real. By paying attention to a few details, and by imagining characters about whom few details even exist, the Bible became real for them—and for us."

"How do you look for such details when it's all you can do to sit down and read the Bible in the first place?" asked the pastor.

"For me it happened when I began helping a classroom of young Russian children read the Bible for the first time," said Helene, "I quickly ran into all kinds of roadblocks. The names of Peter, Mary, Timothy, and Zaccheus meant nothing to them. They were faceless people at best.

"I had an idea. I said to the students, 'When you come to a person's name in the Bible, look for words and phrases that describe him or her. As you read, keep a list of those characteristics or actions. Every time something new jumps out, write it down.'

"At the end of the lesson, one student shared the things he learned about Barnabas:
- 'Joseph, a Levite from Cyprus, whom the apostles called Barnabas (which means Son of Encouragement)'
- 'Sold a field he owned and brought the money and put it at the apostles' feet.'

- 'Took Saul (Paul) to the apostles and "told them how Saul on his journey had seen the Lord and that the Lord had spoken to him, and how in Damascus he had preached fearlessly in the name of Jesus."'
- In Antioch he encouraged the believers in Jerusalem to 'remain true to the Lord with all their hearts.'
- 'He was a good man, full of the Holy Spirit and faith, and a great number of people were brought to the Lord.' (Acts 4:36–37; 9:27; 11:23–24).

"In just a few lines," Helene said, "Barnabas became a real person to this student."

"And," Eugene added, "when the people in the story become real, so does the book you're reading."

Reading with Expectancy

To Helene and Eugene, reading the Word for the first time wasn't a liability at all, but an unexpected blessing. To the visiting American pastor, it was obvious that every time this couple sat down to read the Bible, either to themselves or each other, they fully expected God to reveal something new to them through the Word.

The same curiosity that drove Eugene and Helene to look for revealing details and identify and learn from the Bible's characters also drove them to ask questions. Often, they didn't merely arrive at questions, they thrived on them. Eugene said to the pastor, "The first time I read about Samuel anointing David's head with oil I thought, *Oil? How strange! Why oil?*"

Eugene was not doubting Scripture's authority. Like Helene, he simply wanted to know the God responsible for the Book; it had changed his life.

This was the beauty of approaching the Bible expectantly, yet without expectations. For Helene and Eugene what mattered wasn't how much they already knew, or didn't know, about Scripture, but how their new love for the

Word continually deepened their desire to know and love
God.

"We've never been afraid to ask questions," Helene told
the pastor. "We always want to know more."

Without meaning to, Helene put her finger on yet
another practical insight that can cause a person to experience that moment when understanding and faith come
together in a renewed appreciation of the Word.

*Practical insight number three: The questions you
bring to Scripture may be all that God needs to bring you
to Himself.*

Eugene told the pastor about the day this truth came to
light. "We were reading Paul's familiar words to the
Romans: 'If you confess with your mouth "Jesus is Lord,"
and believe in your heart that God raised him from the
dead, you will be saved' (Rom. 10:9).

"We didn't know what to do with these words," Eugene
said. "At first they were confusing. Why was it so important
to do both—to confess with your mouth and believe with
your heart? God already sees our hearts. Why did we need
to confess with our mouths?

"After we read, we argued for a while, and prayed. Then
we understood that God wants us to unite our mental and
emotional beings in one. He doesn't want us to reject Him
(in our minds), even while we may believe Him (in our
hearts). God needs our minds and our hearts because He
wants all of us! How else can He truly live in us?"

This is how a couple from Minsk became changed forever by a book they thought was dead. God changed Eugene
and Helene in the same way He can change you and me:

- By renewing our minds in unpredictable, piercing
  moments when understanding and faith come
  together.
- By asking questions that lead back to the Book.

- By knowing that the Book, like the characters and Lord it reveals, is as real as the chair in which you sit.
- By finding the forgotten or overlooked detail that can unlock a verse, a story, and a Savior. Again, for the first time.

Going Deeper in the Word

Eugene and Helene's view of God, and their view of the Bible, changed dramatically when they "put themselves in the story." The very things that helped them engage their minds and hearts in the Word are laid out on page 134 of chapter 9.

As you utilize this couple's practical insights, you may discover a new problem, like Yuri Gorban did. Once Yuri picked up the Bible, he couldn't put it down because he found twenty-two surprising lines of Scripture that revealed exactly how God felt about him. They're the same twenty-two verses that could radically alter how you view yourself.

CHAPTER FOUR

Depending Daily on the Word

How the Bible Can Help You Discover Your True Identity

———— ∞ ————

"I praise you, Father, Lord of heaven and earth, because
you have hidden these things from the wise and learned,
and revealed them to little children. Yes, Father, for this
was your good pleasure."

Matthew 11:25

You are chosen of God, holy and dearly loved.

Colossians 3:12, author's paraphrase

You are not your own; you were bought at a price.

1 Corinthians 6:19b–20

It's been said that human existence revolves around
three foundational questions. They are:

- The question of identity: *Who am I?*
- The question of meaning: *Why am I here?*
- The question of direction: *Where am I going?*

Of the three, the most basic question of "Who am I?" may
be the hardest to answer. One reason is that, today, everyone from advertisers to talk-show hosts tells us what we
should buy, how we should act, and, most of all, what we
should think about ourselves. If we didn't know any better,
we would base our identity on what we wear, eat, and

drive. The truth, however, is that we don't really come to discover our true identity—the core of our being—until all that we've come to depend on in this world is taken away. That is what happened to a troubled gang member in northern Russia.

Yuri Gorban found a new way to think about himself and a new way to live when he learned to depend on the one reliable, unchanging source of a person's true identity, the Word of God. This is the story of how he did it, of how an under-utilized approach to Scripture can change a person's life.

He lives in Mariupal, a city of several hundred thousand in northern Russia. On a crisp March morning, Yuri Gorban can feel the sun coming through his tiny bedroom window. While he is yawning, people living in cities like Saint Louis and Phoenix are still asleep. In a few hours they will wake up to the day he has already enjoyed. Yuri gives thanks for simply being alive. He did not always look forward to the sunrise.

He was born in the city of Gonetsk in 1966. For the first few years of his life he was an only child. Today, only a few bruised memories remain: a younger brother and sister crying, a father who was often sad, a mother prodding him to study and to seek a good job. To her and everyone else who wanted good things for him, Yuri said, no. No to school. No to a job. No to life.

The Lie He Believed

Somehow the love that others tried to show him never registered. Running away from home at age eleven, Yuri found his "family" in other runaways. On the street he did not feel so alone. On the street he met other boys his own age. They roamed together, found shelter together, and looked for food together. Those who saw his existence from passing buses and cars thought it was a terrible way to live—to have no parents, no home, no regular meals day after day.

This was how Yuri survived, scrounging for cigarettes and begging for cheap booze. He learned that everything he needed could be his with a little force. His mentors were boys his same age who never had a childhood. Yuri sought them out like a hungry dog in search of meat. Slowly, painfully, he satisfied his appetite for love. One older boy taught him how to fight. Another taught him how to steal. Still another taught him how to kill.

Robbing and fighting was all that Yuri lived for. His heroes were any people stronger than him. To him the epitome of strength was a martial-arts expert and movie star named Bruce Lee, who got everything he wanted—power, money, women, and drugs. Yuri began to live Lee's film fiction—for a price.

He became such a good student of the street that he attracted other, younger boys. They came to him with hungry eyes and no belongings. They came to eat, steal, and roam with their new teacher, so Yuri began to teach them. He talked and they listened. They learned the best way, by example. They would watch him pickpocket and then try it themselves.

Because they hadn't eaten for several days, Yuri's disciples learned very fast. The slightest mistake might bring harm by the fist or the gun. That's why Yuri liked being in control. He liked seeing the look of fear in their eyes. In his mind no one could knock him off. At least that was the lie he let himself believe.

Tears No One Could See

One day Yuri's disciples woke up and found their teacher missing. It was the morning Russian police dragged Yuri to jail for fighting. He was taken to a cement room filled with forty other young men his age. The insides were like a zoo—crowded, smelly, and dirty. To the guards, Yuri was simply another bad animal. Some of the prisoners had homemade knives. Many wanted to kill themselves. Those who wanted to kill Yuri considered his size and then went back to what they were doing.

They couldn't peek under Yuri's facade. They didn't know that underneath the stained T-shirt, behind the scars, Yuri Gorban was just like them. They didn't know that somewhere inside, outside of public view, Yuri Gorban was crying.

Every morning he woke up to feelings of loneliness. Every morning he swallowed hard. Yuri never looked at himself in the mirror. He couldn't stand the sight of his own skin. When he looked at his rough, leathered hands, he saw the pleading faces of people he had silenced. Now their looks haunted him, lived in him, and sorrowed him.

He was a prisoner of his own indecisive feelings. Several years earlier he had gotten married. He had always wanted to be in love with a woman. For a while it felt good, but as the feelings weakened, Yuri disappeared for hours, even days, stealing drugs, taking drugs, staying one step ahead of being caught or killed. At night he would come to bed, sometimes. By then he had no marriage. The only things they had in common were two babies who never saw their father.

Every six months his wife and two daughters came to the jail for a twenty-minute visit. They sat across from Yuri at a table while guards watched and listened to everything they said. No longer did he feel anything for the woman who held his hand. No longer did he know the two restless, little girls who sat across from him.

Yuri looked at his wife and said, "I don't love you anymore. I don't want to live with you anymore. You need to look for another man who can be a good husband to you."

Yuri's wife didn't blink. "I don't want another man," she said. "You are my husband. You are the father of our children. I will wait for you."

When their twenty minutes was up, a guard took Yuri back to his cell. There he laid back down on a metal bunk. He had nothing to live for. He thought he would never again feel happy.

Several years later, though he didn't know how it came about, Yuri Gorban was released from jail. He remembers riding the train to Kiev, looking out the window and seeing the station come into view. As the train slowed, he could see the crowd of people on the platform.

Once the car stopped, Yuri stepped down from the car. There in front of him, emerging from the sea of bodies, was his wife. Next to her were two small, smiling faces. Without thinking, Yuri knelt down, picked them up, and held them to his chest. It was the greatest feeling he'd ever known, until a few days later.

Led by an Angel

That Sunday, Yuri and his family were driving through the city. He saw things he hadn't seen in years—couples holding hands, children riding bicycles, and women watering flowers. Every scene captured his curiosity. One building in particular caught his eye. Though he knew what it was, he said nothing.

He could see the doors were open and people were going inside. Yuri slowed the car to get a better look. For some reason he just wanted to look inside, so Yuri parked the car, and he, his wife, and children went inside the church.

They walked down the long, center aisle and sat in one of the pews toward the back. At the front of the sanctuary a man was preaching about God. Yuri felt the words usher him out of the pew. He stepped to the center aisle and began walking up to the front of the sanctuary. His wife noticed him but did nothing to stop her husband. All the worshipers noticed him. They watched as he walked up to the altar.

Then something happened, something no one else saw or experienced but Yuri himself. He felt someone take his hand and lead him forward. When Yuri turned to see who it was, no one was there. He knew there was only one explanation: an angel had brought him to meet God.

Yuri Gorban stood in front of the sanctuary, alone, and the scenes of his life passed before him. He saw the pain he had caused others. He saw the people he had wronged. He saw ten years of his life in pain, and he wanted it all to go away. He wanted it gone. Instead, the memories welled up until he could no longer hold them inside.

For the first time in his life, alone before the Creator he did not know, Yuri felt his own tears. For twenty-four years he had ignored them, suppressed them, swallowed them, and kept them to himself. Now, all the hurt of his child-hood, the bitterness of the street, and the isolation of prison ran down his cheeks.

The speaker paused. The service stopped. Yuri raised his head, and with his eyes still shut, he heard himself say two words: "Forgive me."

A Child Again

Minutes passed. When Yuri opened his eyes, he saw his wife standing next to him. Something was different inside. He felt younger. He felt innocent again. For the first time, ever, he felt like a child. He thought of his mother and how, years before he went to jail, while he still lived at home, she had changed. It was very personal and very real. All that she said, all that she did, had to do with God and the Bible. In the twenty years since he left home, he had never seen the Book.

Yuri left the church that day aware that his life belonged to God. Three weeks later he and his mother sat down to a homecoming of hugs. As he told her what had happened, she reached over and laid the book he remembered as a child into his hands.

All she said was, "Read, Yuri. You will find your life in these pages. You will find God is alive in these words."

Yuri opened to the first page and began to read. It was so new and so strange. There were people and stories he had never heard of. When he didn't understand the words, he simply kept reading. He read through Genesis, the Psalms, and the Prophets. He didn't want to stop.

Over the next month Yuri read the New Testament, from Matthew to Revelation, fifteen times. Sometimes he sat back and marveled at God. Sometimes he would come to a verse or a story that was worth pondering for a lifetime because the words spoke to the question he had lived with for years, *"Who am I?"* In Paul's letter to the Galatians, Yuri read these words: "I have been crucified with Christ and I no longer live, but Christ lives in me" (Gal. 2:20).

The Yuri Gorban who now gave time and attention to his wife and children, who greeted strangers rather than harassing them, was not really Yuri Gorban! The change went beyond feelings or attitude. The change had to do with his very identity. It was as if God had gutted the very core of his being and had started rebuilding his life from the inside out.

Living his new identity meant leaving the brutality and blood of the streets. It meant finding the courage to look at his past without being bound by it. It meant visiting the gang members he had once tutored. Yuri told them about the change that had taken place in his life. By turning his back on a former way of life and walking toward God, Yuri experienced the true meaning of repentance. It was not a spiritual obligation he had to add to his conversion. Repentance *was* conversion!

This new life, this new identity in Jesus, produced a new, unshakable sense of security. It grew out of a daily habit Yuri began one morning as he sat at his desk. Before the phone began to ring, before the streets became an ocean of noise, while his mind was clear, Yuri simply began reading a short passage of Scripture. Usually it was no more than ten verses.

A Few Minutes Each Day

First he read them silently to himself. As he started reading, he said, "Here I am Lord. I have come to meet You in Your Word. Please speak to me through Your Holy Spirit so that I can know You and serve You today." Almost without exception, as Yuri read the passage over, the words began to find their way into his mind and heart.

By sitting down to read the Word for a few minutes, Yuri was able to get beyond the distractions that had kept him from reading the Bible. *Reading the Scriptures a few minutes each day gave Yuri a growing appreciation for the Word—even at the very point where he was most tempted to quit.*

If he became impatient and wanted to get on with his day, Yuri would ask himself, *Would you get up in the middle of breakfast? Why should spiritual food be any less important? How will you survive if you intentionally try to starve your own spirit?* When Yuri saw reading the Bible not as optional but as *foundational* to his day, he felt free to take as much or as little time as he wanted in the Word.

As the Word became a morning ritual, Yuri wrote this startling discovery: "Everything I have learned about my true worth as a person, my identity in the Lord, has come from reading the Bible on a daily basis. All that I read in the Bible, all that I know myself to be true has deepened over time not because I have kept the Word to myself, but *because I have shared the Scriptures with others."*

As he read the Bible daily, as he learned how God looked at him, accepted him, cherished him, and cared for him, Yuri could not remain quiet. After years of poor self-esteem and low self-acceptance, reading the Word was like sitting down to a meal after going days without food. Like wanting to tell others about an irresistible, home-cooked meal, Yuri couldn't resist telling others where they could find bread.

New Messages of Love

Instead of rushing out to grab people, instead of preaching, Yuri found himself listening to the stories and struggles of people just like himself. These were the people he got to know through casual conversations at work and in his neighborhood.

After hearing their stories, Yuri often sensed that most people were really dealing with life on two different levels. Outwardly, they faced the real pressures of money, family, and jobs. Some had lost their marriages to divorce. Others had lost children to drugs or the street.

However, Yuri detected deeper, unmet needs beneath these exterior issues of life. While remaining sensitive to the other person, he asked a startling question: "Do you know that you are loved?"

At first the person would look shocked, then confused, and often curious. "What do you mean?" they'd ask.

Then Yuri would show them words that they had never before seen: "This is how God showed his love among us: He sent his one and only Son into the world that we might live through him. This is love: not that we loved God, but that he loved us and sent his Son as an atoning sacrifice for our sins. . . . If anyone acknowledges that Jesus is the Son of God, God lives in him and he in God. And so we know and rely on the love God has for us" (1 John 4:9–10,15).

Usually there was a long pause, and Yuri asked a second question: "Do you know these words were written to *you?*

Do you know that right now, right here, God is loving you? It is a fact you can read for yourself."

If the listeners were still curious (and usually they were), Yuri shared the eye-opening truths he had discovered for himself simply by reading the Bible ten minutes a day.

Most people had no idea what to expect. Even Christians who were familiar with some of the statements Yuri read seemed surprised. The Scriptures Yuri shared were, in essence, the message Neil T. Anderson offers in his book *The Bondage Breaker*.[1]

"When you turn your life toward God," said Yuri, "when you find your true identity in Him, this is who you really are: You are Christ's friend (John 15:15). You are a new creation (2 Cor. 5:17). You are God's workmanship, His handiwork, born anew in Christ to do His work (Eph. 2:10). You are an expression of the life of Christ because He is your life (Col. 3:4). You are chosen of God, holy and dearly loved (Col. 3:12)."

Not everyone accepted these words that Yuri read. But those who did, those who claimed these words of Scripture as their own, began to experience the love, acceptance, and forgiveness of God because they had discovered a truth that was central to Yuri's faith.

So Powerless, So Grateful

Twelve months after Yuri came to Christ in front of the sanctuary, a missionary from Russia invited him to take the Bible to the people of Ufa, a city of one million that had but one 1,200-member church. This time Yuri didn't speak to lonely, desperate youth, but to a group of people of all ages in a city park.

---

1. Adapted from Neil T. Anderson, *The Bondage Breaker* (Eugene, Oreg.: Harvest House Publishers, 1990), 229–34.

As Yuri stood before the crowd and prepared to speak, he felt overwhelmed by God's love. It was love that set off a chain reaction of truth.

In and of himself, Yuri realized he was powerless. Once he realized he was powerless, he realized he was helpless; and once he realized he was helpless, Yuri realized who he really was before God—a child.

That day, and over the coming weeks, as he brought the gospel to first-time hearers in new cities across Russia, Yuri Gorban found himself in good company. Consistently, in churches and in parks, wherever he shared the message, the ones who wanted to hear more about Jesus were children.

When he read the Bible, it wasn't the intellectuals or professional people, but children who sat and listened. When it came time to ask questions it wasn't the elderly, the sophisticated, or the rich, but the children who raised their hands. When Yuri read the verses of Scripture that revealed a person's true identity in Christ, the ones who were most eager to hear and willing to believe were children.

Without knowing it, these children had begun to find the answer to the question that every person around the world asks: "Who am I?" God provided the answer in His Word: "Since, then, you have been raised with Christ, set your hearts on things above, where Christ is seated at the right hand of God. Set your minds on things above, not on earthly things. For you died, and your life is now hidden with Christ in God. . . . Therefore, as God's chosen people, holy and dearly loved, clothe yourselves with compassion, kindness, humility, gentleness and patience" (Col. 3:1–3,12).

These are the words that changed Yuri Gorban, words of a Father writing to His children. Words as unchanging as the sunrise. Words to relish and depend on every day. Words that tell you who you really are at the core of your being because of the One who created you from the start.

Going Deeper in the Word

What did you feel inside as you read the verses that described your identity in Christ? encouraged? strengthened? surprised? Imagine discovering a new dimension of God's all-loving nature each time you sit down to read the Word. Later, you'll get a taste of this refreshing approach to Scripture.

Can God still speak to you when the Word is absent, or distant? Three people with convincing evidence think they know.

CHAPTER FIVE

Giving and Receiving the Word

How to Turn to the Bible When You're Either Unwilling or Unable

———∞———

"If you hold to my teaching, you are really my disciples.
Then you will know the truth, and the truth will set you
free."

John 8:32

Forgive as the Lord forgave you.

Colossians 3:13

"The Lord looked down from his sanctuary on high,
    from heaven he viewed the earth,
    to hear the groans of the prisoners
    and release those condemned to death."

Psalm 102:19–20

"I'm facing an impossible situation. I see no way out."

When have you said these words to yourself? When has
a problem seemed so big, so overwhelming, that you
thought not even the Bible could help you?

How can the Word of God speak to you when you're
either unwilling or unable to turn to it? How can you draw
upon the strength of the Lord when you need Him most?

Three Filipino men may know.

Rudy Cantuba, Reggie Opimiano, and Rudy Manzano
each faced an impossible predicament that put their health

and lives at risk. The only reason all three men are alive to tell their story is that they found how simple it is to give someone a copy of the Word, how easy it is to pray the Word, and how basic it is to speak the Word.

In these three small acts of giving and receiving the Scriptures, three ordinary men began a new life of loving God, because they each discovered He was loving them all along.

Rudy Cantuba: The Gift That Opened Him to Life

He was one of the most successful hairstylists in Manila. His clients were the biggest film stars in the Philippines. As a result, Rudy Cantuba had more money and notoriety than he'd ever dreamed of. Yet, it had all come at a price.

"At night I went to clubs, to drink and to feed my nostrils with cocaine. My life was filled with so much tension I had to find some kind of release," said Rudy. "I didn't know how long I could keep up this lifestyle—or keep my secret hidden. I was married. I was the father of four lovely children, and I was gay.

"I had grown up in a family with eight brothers and sisters. At the time I didn't fully understand it, but before I finished grade school I liked playing with girls rather than guys. It was really just a false front to my desire to have a boyfriend.

"My first gay relationship started when I was fifteen. It was sexual attraction, nothing more. After high school the affairs deepened into emotional involvement. No matter how much affection I sought, no matter how much I received, it was never enough. While I kept looking to other men to fill my need for love, my skills and talents in cosmetology took me deeper into the entertainment industry and into the gay scene.

"In 1979 I went to the U.S. to pursue a serious relationship with a man. But once there, everything crumbled. I fell back into drugs and had two serious overdoses. I returned to the Philippines depressed and alone."

Though he found work right away, Rudy admitted, "I didn't know what I was looking for. When I started new gay relationships, guys would leave. I felt so embarrassed, and I felt so much pain inside. I tried to commit suicide. I had money, a good job, and fame, but I felt so restless inside I thought I was going insane.

"I began to wonder about getting married, but I thought, *Who would marry me?* How could I be a man when my heart was not ready to fall in love with a woman?"

A woman who was a regular customer of Rudy's began talking to him during an appointment. This time he showed more interest than usual. A month later, Rudy and Esther were married.

"All I thought about was using her as a cover-up," admitted Rudy. "I wanted to prove to myself I was a man. I wanted to believe I could *make* myself different and love a woman."

However, nothing changed. While Esther raised the couple's twin boys, Rudy became involved with a gay married man. She had no idea it was going on until one night he knocked on their front door. When Rudy opened the door, he turned to Esther and said, "This is my boyfriend."

What was left of their marriage dissolved into a set of weekly calendar appointments. Rudy and Esther reserved Monday, Tuesday, and Wednesday nights at home with their children. Friday and Saturday nights were reserved for Rudy and his boyfriend. Feasting on professional accolades, Rudy won the highest award in international hairdressing. "Onlookers and friends thought I was on top of the world. Inside, I knew I was still living in a pit of hopelessness."

Rudy kept going, enduring his marriage, developing his gay love affair, and feeling miserable. He had no idea his life was about to change.

New Reading Assignment

"It was a very busy day in the salon," Rudy recalled. "I was finishing a permanent for a woman I had known for several years. Her name was Kate Garcia, and she knew my whole story. She knew of my lovers, my temptations, and my tears. She knew I was suffering from heart trouble. It was serious enough that my doctor wanted to do surgery and insert a pacemaker.

"I don't know how it came about, but as the conversation was winding down Kate turned to me and said, 'Rudy, there's something I've been wanting to give you.' I looked up from the woman's hair I was working on and saw Kate holding a Bible. She set it on the counter next to a mirror. 'Read it when you have time,' Kate said. 'There's a lot inside.'

"I thanked her politely and didn't think a thing about it. That night I took the Bible home and put it by a stack of old magazines. It stayed there for weeks until one day, while Esther was gone, I reached down and started reading.

"I had never owned a Bible, so after a few pages I had all kinds of questions. *What should I read? What does this book have to do with me?* I thought.

The First Commandment

Rudy turned to the Book of Exodus. In chapter 20 he came to the Ten Commandments. He got as far as the first two, and stopped: "You shall have no other gods before me. You shall not make for yourself an idol in the form of anything in heaven above or on the earth beneath or in the waters below. You shall not bow down to them or worship them; for I the LORD your God, am a jealous God, punishing the children for the sin of the fathers to the third and fourth generation of those who hate me, but showing love to a thousand generations of those who love me and keep my commandments" (Exod. 20:3–6).

"When I read these words something stirred inside me. I couldn't explain it—and I couldn't get the words out of my mind. Though I didn't know God, I heard Him speaking to me in what I had read.

"These words were real because they described my life. Three nights of the week I masqueraded as a loving husband and father. The other two nights I satisfied my lusts. In the anxious moments in between, I debated how to take my own life.

"I wanted to be free of my sexual desires for men, but I didn't know how. Since I couldn't escape these urges, since I couldn't conquer them by myself, I had come to accept them. Marriage, willpower, and counseling—none of it had worked for me.

"By reading the Bible I learned the real causes of homosexuality and why I had become gay. When I read the words the Lord had given Moses, it was clear to me that my homosexuality was not the fault of my parents. I didn't blame them or anyone else.

"Homosexuality, my homosexuality, was the consequence of human beings' idolatry. Homosexuality, *my* homosexuality, was the consequence of the sin of gay men who worshiped not God but each other. In my homosexual acts I had idolized other men. They, in turn, idolized and worshiped me with their bodies. In our worship of each other, we worshiped creatures rather than the Creator; I had made an unnatural physical relationship with other men more important than God."

Changed by the Word

For the first time in years, perhaps for the first time in his life, Rudy Cantuba felt different about himself. In his most desperate moment, he experienced an unmistakable peace and he knew the reason why.

"When I read the Bible, I found something new, something I never had before. When I read the Bible, I found the wisdom and strength of God. When I had the wisdom and strength of God, I experienced life, *His* life in me.

"In the Bible I found the living Lord convicting me, forgiving me, and freeing me from myself. By drawing upon the Word I found I was living the promise of Jesus when He said, 'If you hold to my teaching, you are really my disciples. Then you will know the truth, and the truth will set you free' [John 8:31–32]."

When his boyfriend came to the house a few days later, Rudy told him their relationship was over. From that day on, he began to rebuild his marriage. Later that same year he began to serve God in a way he never imagined, as a church pastor.

Rudy Cantuba's life changed forever through the simple gesture of another person who cared. "I might still be feeling the pain of destructive relationships and drugs if Kate Garcia hadn't given me a Bible. When my life was at the brink, she did the one thing I couldn't do for myself. She gave me the greatest, permanent expression of God's love I could ever know. She gave me His Word when I needed it most."

One of the simplest, most direct ways to receive the Word and know its power, as Rudy Cantuba discovered, is to read it whenever it's within your reach.

Rudy received the Word because a friend simply gave him his own copy of the Bible.

Reggie Opimiano:
The Choice to Pray, The Chance to Forgive

Like Rudy Cantuba, Reggie Opimiano was able to draw upon the Word when he needed it most because someone did something even more basic than giving the Word. In his hour of greatest need, Reggie received the truth and power of Scripture because his wife knew how to pray the Word.

Reggie was in his fourth year of high school military training. The class had been hard, the hours long. More than once he had stepped out of line, and more than once his instructors ordered him to do push-ups and laps around the track. Each time Reggie obliged. Each time his silent anger fueled a quiet rage.

One morning the officer ordered Reggie to get down on the ground and do two hundred push-ups in front of his classmates.

"I walked forward as if I was going to get down on the ground," recalled Reggie, "but instead, I lunged at him. I grabbed the forty-five caliber pistol he wore around his waist. Before he could react I turned the gun on him and fired. The other lieutenant was inches away, so I aimed at him and pulled the trigger. Then I ran for my life."

As two Filipino army officers lay dead, Reggie fled the school grounds and disappeared into the waterfront. That night, as police officers sliced the night air with flashlights, Reggie hid deep in the belly of a ship bound for Manila.

When the freighter arrived in port four days later, the police were waiting with handcuffs. The courts wasted no time. The trial took only a few hours. For killing two people, Reggie Opimiano was sentenced to fifteen years in prison.

One, Solitary Miracle

He quickly adjusted to his new surroundings. Six months after he arrived, Reggie organized a riot in which six inmates died. During the struggle he took one guard hostage and killed another with a homemade knife. For the next seven years Reggie lived in complete isolation.

Before he entered solitary, Reggie had found a Bible. "For some reason I started reading it. It was the only way I came to know that God exists. I learned things I never knew. Even though I had killed three people, I learned that God loved and forgave me before I was even born. Though I was in prison, I learned that this God still wanted good things for me.

"In solitary I had just the clothes on my back. Even though my Bible was eventually taken away, I began to change. I felt the terrible weight of guilt and shame begin to lift. I began to pray. I prayed, 'God, release me from this place. Release me from myself.'"

Amazingly, just moments later, Reggie heard his name on the prison intercom: "Reggie Opimiano, come to the warden's office." A guard opened his cell door and said, "You are no longer in isolation. You are released to the main population."

"Though I was still a convicted murderer, a feeling of thankfulness poured over me. Though I was still in prison, I knelt down and thanked God for my new freedom." Over the next nine years Reggie read and studied the Bible, unaware that he was preparing himself for the day he would need God's Word to save him from himself.

Revenge!

It came not long after his final release from prison. He had become a church pastor and had begun a new life with a woman he had married while still a prisoner. One afternoon, while Reggie was working at the church, his wife, Carmen, was leading a Bible study in their home. After all the people had left, Carmen began scrubbing the laundry while their four-and-a-half-year-old daughter slept in her bedroom.

However, everyone had *not* left the house. After she finished cleaning, Carmen went to check on her daughter and discovered she had not taken her regular nap. Instead she sat curled up in a ball in the corner of her room, traumatized and crying.

She threw her arms around her mother. Then in short, nervous stutterings she told her mother what had happened: A man who had attended the Bible study crept silently into her bedroom and raped her.

When Reggie came home he found his wife and daughter holding each other, crying. When he heard the news, the anger of his youth spewed out like uncontrolled fire. One way or another he would get revenge.

That afternoon Reggie bought a gallon of gas. He knew where the man lived. He planned to set the man's house on fire that night. Reggie's wife sensed her husband's rage. She fell to her knees and said, "Don't you see, we're the ones suffering. Why don't you give your anger to God?"

Reggie refused. That night Carmen didn't know her husband planned to carry out his revenge at three o' clock in the morning. When he came to bed, Reggie set the full gas can outside their back door and put a new pistol with twenty-four new bullets under his pillow.

Before Carmen turned over and fell asleep, she said, "Reggie, leave it with God. Your background and your anger are still with you. If you do anyone any harm, your testimony as a pastor will be destroyed."

While his wife slept, Reggie remained awake. At two-thirty he looked at his watch. At three o' clock he thought about getting dressed. Then, Carmen did something she had never done before. Minutes before Reggie planned to leave the house, she woke up. She sat up on one elbow and said, "Reggie, will you please pray with me that you will not burn the home of this man and his family. Don't take revenge. Take your feelings, take yourself, to God."

His Greatest Hour of Need

Against his will, against his feelings of uncontrollable anger, Reggie Opimiano began to pray. He prayed words of Scripture he had read and mulled over for eighteen years.

As he prayed God's words, he began to find the words for his bitterness and hatred.

"After praying for several minutes, my mind became clear. The anger that was so intense moments ago went away. For the first time since I hugged my little girl hours after she was raped, I felt peaceful. It was a peace I could not describe." By praying the Word, Reggie Opimiano received the peace and presence of God in his hour of greatest need.

In the darkness of early morning, Carmen turned to her husband and said, "Let's go to the police tomorrow and tell them what we know so they can carry out their investigation." The next morning they did. Three hours later, police arrested the man who had raped the Opimiano's daughter, and that day he confessed to his crime.

Early on in the trial, the man's mother and father came to Reggie, filled with remorse for what their son had done. Not knowing Reggie had served seventeen years in prison, they said to him, "You know that, if convicted, our son will never get out of prison. Please, please forgive him. You can plead mercy with the judge."

Reggie looked at them and said, "I know someone who once was in prison, and he felt he would never be free. You are looking at him. Today I am free because God's love and forgiveness in Christ are greater than the murders I committed." Reggie asked the judge that the convicted man not serve his full sentence, but that he be allowed to start his life over in a new town. The judge agreed.

By receiving the Word, Carmen knew how to pray the Word. By praying the Word, Carmen saw her husband come to renewed faith; by receiving the Word, Reggie was able to receive and extend the same forgiveness Christ had shown him; he was able to live the Word: "Forgive as the Lord forgave you" (Col. 3:13).

Rudy Manzano: Sentenced to Life

There's at least a third way to draw upon the power of God's Word when you're either unwilling or unable. It's as simple as putting a Bible in someone's hands, as basic as praying the Bible during someone's hour of greatest need.

Innocent

It happened to Rudy Manzano after being convicted of a crime he didn't commit. He and his cousin were walking back from a local fish market when, out of nowhere, a stranger began hurling insults at the two. The cousin barked back. Tempers rose, and in a swirl of fists the stranger pulled out a knife.

Rudy ran home to find a gun to protect himself. When he returned he found the stranger dead on the ground. Standing over him was Rudy's uncle, who had been walking home when he was pulled into the melee. In self-defense he had killed the man. Of all the innocent bystanders who arrived on the scene too late to be eyewitnesses, none was more shocked than Rudy.

Though the uncle admitted to the murder, during the trial, police read statements from onlookers who said Rudy was the killer! The victim's family agreed. Unbelievably, Rudy was convicted of murder and sentenced to death by electrocution.

"I went to prison fully expecting to die," said Rudy. "The only thing I lived for was my wife and a new baby daughter. They meant more to me than anything, more than God, the Bible, or prayer. I'd been taught to believe in all three, but deep down I doubted them all."

He doubted the words of a visiting friend who had brought him a Bible to read. "There's hope for you, Rudy," the young man told Rudy. "The verdict handed down is not yet final. There is injustice in the human court, but there is justice in the heavenly court."

Needed: One Blood Donor

Rudy was still dubious when, several months later, a Christian worker inside the prison came to him saying, "I need your help. A friend of mine is in need of blood; she needs an operation. Unless she receives blood, she'll die."

Since he was going to die anyway, Rudy thought, why not help someone live? On the appointed day, Rudy pumped his hand so hard the nurse ordered him to stop. That day the Christian worker came by and said, "I want you to know, Rudy, that nothing is impossible with God. Nothing." Rudy shrugged his shoulders. He didn't know if the person who needed his blood lived or died. He wasn't sure he even cared.

Four months later, the same Christian worker was back at the prison. This time he came with a group of women. They invited Rudy to a small worship service, and out of politeness he agreed to go.

As they walked into the chapel the worker said, "I'd like you to meet someone, Rudy. This is Raquel, the woman who needed your blood."

The petite woman smiled at Rudy. "I want to thank you for what you did. Several weeks ago I had an operation for a tumor. Without someone's blood I wouldn't have been able to live. Will you sit beside me in the service?"

The two sat down together in one of the pews as the pastor stood up and began to speak. "All of us are worthy of the sentence of death," he said. "There is one here, today, who though he committed no sin, was illegally tried and sentenced to die."

Rudy couldn't believe what he was hearing. *I know who he's talking about,* he thought to himself. *He's talking about me.*

The pastor continued. "Though he was sentenced to die, in his willingness to help people he gave himself."

Rudy's mind raced: *Sentenced to die. . . . A willingness to help others. . . . I know this person!* he thought, smiling to himself.

Then the pastor said, "This person is here today. The one who was sentenced unjustly to die, who gave His blood willingly, who loved others and loves you."

At that moment Rudy Manzano knew exactly whom the pastor was talking about, and it was not him, but another person who had been sentenced unjustly, and who had given His blood because He desired to help others. Rudy Manzano stopped thinking about himself long enough to think of the person he had read about in the Bible. That night he stepped from doubt to faith and found the words he had never been able to say, "Lord, tonight I trust You with my life."

Because someone spoke the written Word, Rudy Manzano was able to receive the Living Word. Only because of this was Rudy able to turn to the Word when he needed it the most. That took place while Rudy was still on death row. When he learned his wife was divorcing him, he prayed, "My hope is all gone. I have no one to turn to, now, but You, Lord."

When he ran out of words to pray, Rudy began reading Psalm 102: "The LORD looked down from his sanctuary on high, from heaven he viewed the earth, to hear the groans of the prisoners and release those condemned to death" (Ps. 102:19–20).

"Lord, if I could write words to You, this is exactly what I'd say." Rudy wrote the psalm on his cell door. For the next eleven months they became his prayer and his hope until one day a guard brought Rudy a letter from the Supreme Court of the Philippines. The message was very clear and very short.

After reviewing his case, the judges ruled that Rudy had been violated, unconstitutionally, in his sentencing. He had been charged with homicide, but convicted of murder. To

convict and punish a person of a crime more severe than
that with which he had been charged was a violation of his
constitutional rights. "Therefore," the last sentence read,
"it is so ruled that Rudy Manzano is hereby released from
the Manila Federal Penitentiary."

Rudy looked up and read the words on the wall of his
cell: "The LORD looked down from his sanctuary on high,
from heaven he viewed the earth, to hear the groans of the
prisoners and release those condemned to death."

It was more than a promise fulfilled; it was the beginning
of a new life.

Going Deeper in the Word

Today, Rudy Manzano, Reggie Opimiano, and Rudy Cantuba are all pastors. Each has dedicated his life to telling
others about the One they found: in a pastor who spoke the
Word; in a faithful wife who prayed the Word; in a caring
person who put the Word within her friend's grasp.

This is how you can turn to the Word and find hope, forgiveness, and a new beginning—by receiving the Word
when you least expect it, and then by giving to others the
Christ you can't keep to yourself.

What would happen if you shared your experience with
God with someone you know? Maybe it's a friend you've met
recently at school, work, a church gathering, or an aerobic
exercise class. It could be someone right in your immediate
or extended family. What would happen if you used the words
of Scripture as your prayer of love and concern for this person? What would happen if you gave this person a Bible?

Speaking, praying, and actually giving the Word to someone you know might feel a little risky. In chapter 9, you'll
see how receiving and giving the Word through practical
acts of caring can be freeing. If that happens, you'll know
what it means to cherish God's Word just like four extraordinary people on the other side of the world who've risked
everything.

CHAPTER SIX

Cherishing the Word

How the Bible Can Bring Unspeakable Joy

———∞———

> For I have learned to be content whatever the circumstances. I know what it is to be in need, and I know what it is to have plenty. I have learned the secret of being content in any and every situation, whether well fed or whether living in plenty or in want. I can do everything through him who gives me strength.
>
> Philippians 4:11–13

Today, two thousand years after they were written, Paul's words to the Philippians are alive in a country where thousands of people each day are hearing and believing the gospel for the first time. In their part of the world, the spread of Christianity is so rapid, the demand for the Word so great, that in some places there are only one or two Bibles for every one thousand new believers.

Despite ongoing government surveillance, persecution, imprisonment, and, at times, physical beatings, one thing has sustained them, the Word of God. By cherishing the Word, each of these remarkable people has experienced life-changing joy. One is a taxi driver who talked a passenger out of suicide over the course of a ride "around the block" that lasted three hours. The second is a world-class scholar who rejected an offer to earn 130 times her annual salary by teaching at a prestigious American university.

The third is a pastor who was arrested in the middle of his sermon and who, within a few weeks, transformed the lives of his twenty cellmates living in a cell built for ten. The fourth is an itinerant evangelist who travels fifty weeks a year to reach thousands of people who have never heard the name "Jesus."

Each of these people has been sustained, renewed, and strengthened by the Word. Though they live on the other side of the world, they've discovered a joy that you and I can know right where we live—the invisible reality of Christ who lives in us "in any and every situation, whether well fed or hungry, whether living in plenty or in want" (Phil. 4:12).

To know the joy of these four distinctive individuals is to know their home—the enigmatic, complex, and beautiful country called China.

The Taxi Driver: One Startling Ride

On the hot, muggy afternoon of June 3, 1989, Wang Cheng looked out over Beijing's Tiananmen Square and tried to comprehend a sight he'd never seen: thousands of Chinese standing together as one in defiance of their country's Communist government. Less than a hundred yards away, soldiers, armed with guns, lined both sides of Tiananmen Street ready to confront protesters who refused to move.

For most of his life, Brother Wang, a twenty-nine-year-old taxi driver, had revered and respected the Communists. His father had served in the Communist army. When Brother Wang was ten years old, he wanted to fight for the Communists. In school and at home he was taught to believe that Communism was the only thing that would save China and the world.

As he grew older, Brother Wang felt more and more uncomfortable with how the Communists wanted to control his life. They wanted to control what he and his countrymen could and could not believe. They wanted to control what he and his friends could and could not say in public. They wanted to control what he and his family members could and could not do for work. Such restrictions had left Brother Wang feeling empty and unsatisfied. The Communists could make bold pronouncements about political beliefs, but they couldn't speak to his own hopes and desires for life.

In the days that preceded the growing tension in Tiananmen Square, Brother Wang had become sympathetic with the crowd of student demonstrators. Even though he had never experienced freedom, he wanted it. Even though he wasn't sure where the students' slogans and speeches would lead, Brother Wang admired their courage.

In the restless hours after midnight on June 4, Brother Wang was at a friend's house, just a few miles away from Tiananmen Square, when Communist troops opened fire on the crowd. Five thousand men and women, most of them students, died that night. Twice as many lay wounded. By the time the sun came up, all the dead bodies had been dragged away, all the blood stains had been scoured. The next morning Tiananmen Square looked strangely empty, as if nothing had happened; but Brother Wang, like most Chinese, knew otherwise.

"My faith in Communism died that night," he told his friend. "After the Tiananmen Square massacre, I'm not sure what to believe about my country, or my future."

Though deeply disillusioned, Brother Wang continued driving his taxi through the streets of Beijing. In the daily stream of passengers who shared his world for five or ten minutes at a time, one man stood out. He told a story Brother Wang had never heard. It was the almost-unbelievable story of a God who came to earth as a human being. The man carried a book Brother Wang had never seen before. As he maneuvered through traffic, Brother Wang listened, both startled and intrigued by the things the man said and read.

Brother Wang and his passenger represented two distinct traditions in China. The passenger's lineage went back hundreds of years when eager, European traders, led by Marco Polo, began exploring new avenues of trade in Asia. Their destination was the isolated, self-sufficient culture called China.

What they brought back to Europe were valuable silks, spices, and teas—and the perplexing discovery that they had nothing in the way of material goods to interest the Chinese as a trading partner—but the Europeans could not leave this new, unexplored region of the world alone. Since the Chinese had no open markets, the Europeans decided to create one. The crop they introduced to a wary Asian culture was opium. Over the years, the Chinese bought it and smoked it. Once the Chinese became addicted to a drug they had never wanted or sought, the Western world had the economic inroad it needed.

It was within this soiled context that modern-day Christian missionaries made their way into China. The only way missionary pioneers like Hudson Taylor could get into China was on river gunboats that carried Western traders into the country's interior. It was Taylor and others who brought some of the first translations of the Chinese Bible. The passenger sitting in Brother Wang's taxi, who freely talked about a Jesus millions of Chinese still knew nothing about, was one of those spiritual descendants.

Brother Wang drew his identity from a contrasting lineage of twentieth-century politics. Brother Wang's heritage had been shaped by the Communists' 1949 overthrow of the Kuomintang government. The event sowed the seeds of socialism that eventually gave rise to Mao Zedong's Cultural Revolution of the mid 1960s with its harsh crackdown of all of the country's religious activities. Thirty years later, the China that Brother Wang knew was a culture of limited freedoms and crumbling national hopes. In the shadow of the Tiananmen horror, Brother Wang faced a dilemma. He could no longer trust the Communists, and he could not give his allegiance to the God revealed in the book of his passenger.

Brother Wang, however, was too curious. Over the next several stop-and-go miles he asked the man to tell him more about his beliefs. When it came time for him to get out, the passenger paid his fare. Then he put the only Bible he had ever owned into Brother Wang's hands and said, "You must have this. You must read this. Then, you must call me so we can talk."

Brother Wang was shocked. That day his work could not end soon enough. That night he started reading. As he read, he found himself believing the God whose nature, purposes, and plans unfolded in this collection of poems, letters, and eyewitness accounts.

As Brother Wang placed his faith in the God the "new" Book, he soon had a problem: he could not keep silent about what he read. He knew that if he told his passengers about Christianity he could be arrested and put in jail, but he took the risk. Usually the conversations lasted only several blocks. One day, however, things got a little out of control.

The passenger had climbed in nervously and said, "Just drive." For dozens of city blocks Brother Wang listened to a man pour out his life of drug addiction and suicide attempts. As Brother Wang listened he prayed silently. He asked God what to do. Brother Wang showed the man the new book he had come to cherish, "Not long ago someone gave me this to read. Let me tell you what it says." Brother Wang read, "'Come to me, all you who are weary and burdened, and I will give you rest'" (Matt. 11:28). Then Brother Wang read another claim of Jesus: "'I am the resurrection and the life. He who believes in me will live, even though he

dies; and whoever lives and believes in me will never die'"
(John 11:25–26).

"Do you believe this?" he asked his passenger. The man's
response went on for the next sixty city blocks. Three hours
after their ride began, the passenger reached his destination. As he turned to get out of the taxi, there were tears in
his eyes. He looked at Brother Wang and said, "You have
what I want." Brother Wang then handed the man his Bible,
the Bible he had been given, the only Bible he had ever
seen.

As Brother Wang drove away he noticed the business-
man had given him double the fare for three hours of driving. The amount was worth one week's pay. To Brother
Wang, it could not begin to equal what had just happened:
The God of the Bible had come alive in a person for the first
time.

This is what joy looks like on the streets of Beijing. The
joy of being used by God to give someone the hope, the
Jesus, the Book they've never known. When that opportunity comes along for you, and it will, you'll have a choice to
make, just like a woman named Yang Meng.

The University Scholar: One Unforgettable Student

Sister Chen put down the letter and looked out the window of her small office at one of China's leading universi-
ties, where she enjoyed the reputation of being a world-
class researcher in her field. The letter in front of her was
not the first she had received from a prestigious American
university. Like the others, this was an invitation to accept
a full professorship in the U.S. Sister Chen looked at the
starting annual salary: $52,000, or 416,000 Chinese yuan,
130 times her current annual salary. What was she going
to do?

Sister Chen had grown up as an only child. Her parents
had heard the gospel from Chinese missionaries. There

had never been a day in her life when she didn't know the Lord. Not a week passed that she didn't read Scripture verses given to her by Chinese church leaders who didn't even own their own Bible.

Now, in her mid-thirties, Sister Chen lived alone in a small, one-bedroom apartment. She owned just three dresses and one pair of shoes. Her most valuable possession was a used, single-speed bicycle. After she paid for rent, food, and a few personal items each month, she gave what little money she had left to her church and her graduate students.

Whenever she wondered if it was right for her to teach in the U.S., she thought about them. And after considering each offer, after praying earnestly for days, she had decided, each time, to remain in China. Now, she wondered once again. The deadline to respond to the American professor was two days away.

That night, like every night, was the same for her. Instead of visiting friends or relaxing, Sister Chen welcomed graduate students into her living room. She knew the university encouraged and expected scholarship. She knew, too, that her colleagues and superiors would be angry if they ever found out what she had been doing for months. After working on a current assignment, Sister Chen and her students did what none of her university colleagues would ever permit: quietly, together, Sister Chen and her graduate students studied the Bible.

Sister Chen knew it was a risk. She knew that if her department chairman ever found out how much time she spent studying "the collected myths called Christianity," her job, her career in teaching, could end.

Students like Li Hun were the reason Sister Chen kept her heart open to God and to His Word. Three weeks earlier, after months of examining and debating the Scriptures with Brother Li, this brilliant, young graduate student had accepted the Lord. "I want to know everything you know about Jesus—and more," he told her. After days of asking friends in secret, Sister Chen found a Bible for Brother Li. From that day on, the Book was never out of his sight.

Sister Chen had been home for less than an hour one night when Brother Li phoned. "Is it time to study?" he asked.

"In twenty minutes," she replied. Sister Chen and her students were careful not to reveal their true purpose for meeting on the phone. She knew government officials had ways of listening in and making life miserable for those they chose to pressure.

When Brother Li came to her apartment, he immediately shut the door, took out his Bible, and opened it to the story of Jesus' first miracle at the wedding in Cana. Brother Li could not contain his curiosity. "Just when did the water become wine?" he asked his professor.

Sister Chen didn't know what to say. *Why not look at the passage*, she thought, *and let the Holy Spirit lead them?*

"Let's read the account aloud," she said to Brother Li.

> On the third day a wedding took place at Cana in Galilee. Jesus' mother was there, and Jesus and his disciples had also been invited to the wedding. When the wine was gone, Jesus' mother said to him, "They have no more wine."
>
> "Dear woman, why do you involve me?" Jesus replied, "My time has not yet come."
>
> His mother said to the servants, "Do whatever he tells you."
>
> Nearby stood six stone water jars, the kind used by the Jews for ceremonial washing, each holding from twenty to thirty gallons.
>
> Jesus said to the servants, "Fill the jars with water"; so they filled them to the brim.
>
> Then he told them, "Now draw some out and take it to the master of the banquet."
>
> They did so, and the master of the banquet tasted the

water that had been turned into wine. He did not realize where it had come from, though the servants who had drawn the water knew. (John 2:1–9)

Having prayed for the Holy Spirit to lead them, Sister Chen said, "You wonder when the water first became wine. I believe that whatever the answer is—and we may not know—our not knowing does not change the truth of Jesus and the Word. In fact, it's fair to assume there were probably people at the wedding who may not have believed in Jesus."

Brother Li pointed to the passage: "The master of the banquet tasted the water that had been turned to wine. Is it possible the water may have turned to wine the moment he first tasted? Is it possible," he asked, "that faith becomes real when we first believe Jesus?

"Three weeks ago I was that person who had never 'tasted.' Today I know Jesus, I believe Jesus, because I have His Word. You, Professor Meng, showed me this Jesus because you showed me His Book, the Bible.

"You know I have Christian friends who cannot do what I am doing here with you. They cannot read the Word; they cannot know the Word; they cannot study the Word; they cannot love the Word—because they do not have a copy of this Word for themselves."

Sister Chen shared Brother Li's sadness. She knew the only "Bible" some students had was the handful of verses they had committed to memory. That evening, after Brother Li left her apartment, Sister Chen thought of the other students she had tried to encourage and teach. For every person like Brother Li she knew there were many other Christians at her university, in her city, and throughout China who had never seen the Word.

That night, after Brother Li left, she sat down at her desk and wrote her response to the U.S. professor:

Dear Sir,

Thank you for the distinction of being invited to join your respected faculty and to come teach at your school. I regret that I cannot accept your invitation. While I am honored by your offer, there are unfinished commitments I must fulfill here in China.

This is how cherishing the Word leads to joy, the joy of watching another person come to a deeper love of the Living Word and the written Word. When that opportunity comes along for you, and it will, you may be blessed with giving a little bit more of yourself than you expected, just like a pastor named Wo Chao discovered.

The Pastor: One Remarkable Reunion

The most unforgettable Sunday of his life started out like any other. Wo Chao stood inside the small house and welcomed men, women, and youth who had walked for miles to attend that morning's worship service. They came to hear readings from the Book none of them owned. They came to pray and sing hymns. They came to worship God, knowing full well their meeting was strictly forbidden by local officials. Brother Chao knew the threat was real because he knew history.

Brother Chao wasn't yet born when the Communists came to power in 1949. Their takeover, which left thousands dead, had sent shivers through China's church. To stifle Christianity's spiraling growth, the Communists expelled all of the country's foreign missionaries and imprisoned virtually all Chinese pastors. To tighten their hold on religious activity, the Communists took over China's indigenous, or "Three-Self," church that had developed in the wake of the Boxer Rebellion of 1900. The name symbolized the desire of the Chinese to be self-supporting, self-propagating, and self-governing.

In the 1950s, the Communists added an "antiforeigner" patriotic element and thus, the Three-Self Patriotic Movement, or TSMP, was born. Though some pastors joined the movement, most Chinese Christians saw through the political motive. They refused to go along with an atheistic government that dictated when and where they could meet and what they could and could not preach, read, and teach. Reverend Wang Mingdao was one such Christian leader.

Throughout the 1930s and 40s, Wang had been a popular itinerant evangelist in China. In 1954, officials held a public meeting in Beijing to denounce Wang. The public refused to support the government's claims against Wang, and the evangelist continued to preach. A year later, after still refusing to register his own congregation as a TSMP church, he was arrested again and sent to prison. After a year of intense coercion and persecution, Wang finally relented to officials. Contrary to every fiber in his being, he agreed to join the Three-Self Movement. It was a huge coup for the government, for in Wang they had captured the allegiance of a major Christian leader revered by thousands of believers.

Wang could not live with himself. Believing he had denied his Lord and the gospel, he went back to the officials and reneged on his agreement with them. Against their wishes, he said he would continue to preach and have nothing to do with the TSMP, its vision, programs, or people. He never got the chance to fulfill this promise. For giving his total allegiance to Jesus Christ rather than the TSMP, Wang spent the next twenty-two years in prison.

His persecution lit a fire under thousands of Chinese Christians who refused to take part in the Three-Self Movement. Instead they began meeting in houses to worship and pray and read the Word, free from government restrictions. By 1990 the number of Chinese Christians had soared to 75 million.

Brother Chao's conversion, like the church's growth, was dramatic and unforeseen. For two weeks he had been severely ill. He laid on his back in a hospital bed, unable to open his mouth, when Christians visiting other patients came to his room. "If you believe Jesus," they said, "you will be healed." Brother Chao believed. Four days later his illness went away completely.

During this time Brother Chao heard God say to him, "You have to preach my Word and witness to others." Brother Chao did. Everything the Communists had said was illegal—including praying, reading, and preaching the Word—were the very things Brother Chao began to do as a pastor and church planter. These were the very things he was preparing to do that Sunday morning as three strangers in police uniforms walked into the house-church worship service.

Swiftly, without words, they grabbed Brother Chao by the arms. As startled believers looked on, officials handcuffed him. For preaching the gospel, Brother Chao was led off to jail. The worshipers rose to their feet and shouted angrily at the officials. Realizing the futility of their own words, they began to pray that God would be with their pastor and bring good out of his jail sentence.

For the next four hours, police beat Brother Chao's left leg with a wooden club. It had happened before, after other arrests. This time, however, the pain was worse than anything he had ever felt. "Give me the strength to last, oh God," he prayed. "Keep me faithful so that one day I can take your Word to others."

With his leg swollen and bleeding, Brother Chao was pushed into a cell made for ten inmates. Inside were twenty men. The only way each one could fully stretch out to sleep that night was if they slept head to foot.

In the morning Brother Chao received the first of two meager, daily meals: a small ball of rice no bigger than his fist. For the next twelve hours, from the first rays of sunlight to the gray silence of night, Brother Chao and his cell-mates sat huddled on the cold cement floor. While the others looked despondent, Brother Chao recalled the words God spoke to Joshua: "As I was with Moses, so I will be with you; I will never leave you or forsake you" (1:5).

By the end of the first day, he had shared these words freely with his cellmates. Brother Chao taught them hymns and gave them words, like those from Joshua. By the end of the first week, all twenty knelt down and prayed before each meal.

Every week Brother Chao was beaten with various blunt objects—broom handles, thin sticks, or rods. Every day he prayed for the strength to remain faithful to his Lord. One day, without warning, his prayer was interrupted when guards appeared in front of his cell. They opened the metal door and told him to step outside. Without any explanation, they pointed to the front door. After five months in jail, Brother Chao was free.

That morning there was no question in Brother Chao's mind what he would do first. He staggered down the road, barely able to walk, holding on to his still-swollen legs, still weak and wobbly from the beatings. Four hours later, after walking six miles, Brother Chao reached his village where grateful friends embraced him.

Brother Chao told them he needed money. The people responded generously. Brother Chao then walked to a nearby market, where he used all the money to buy cookies, fruits, and dumplings. He put all the items in a sack, put the sack on his back, and began the six-mile walk back to the jail.

It was near midnight when the jail guard noticed a familiar-looking man standing at the door. He stared at Brother Chao and asked, "What are you doing back here?"

"I had to come back; my friends are here. I've come to bring them food. Would you please give them all that's in this bag? And please tell them it is from me?" Though still befuddled, the guard agreed.

What hurt Brother Chao more than his sore legs was the realization that he could not see his friends. Yet his disappointment did not last long. That week he returned to preach at the house church where he had been arrested. Again it was filled with people, and standing in the small room were some of the men in the cell with whom he had prayed, eaten, and shared the Word. Brother Chao thought of them as he preached about another ex-prisoner named Paul: "God has been good to me. He has protected me. He has given me a surprising peace, peace that I cannot understand" (Phil. 4:7, author's paraphrase).

This is the sound of joy in the house churches of China. This is joy that shines through antagonism, confinement, and physical pain, that captures people and frees them to know the "secret of being content in any and every situation" (Phil. 4:12).

The Evangelist: One Enduring Vision

A woman named Su Zhang learned the secret of being content. By sitting down to read the Bible with two common items, her life changed forever.

She was just sixteen years old at the time. Normally Sister Zhang would have been at school in the forested region of southern China. Instead she found herself at home caring for her mother, who lay in bed with chronic headaches. After several days the pain began to increase. Traditional Chinese herbal medicine had not worked. The outlook was not good.

Sister Zhang's despondency was interrupted one day when she heard a knock at the door and met a stranger, a woman who obviously wanted to talk. Sister Zhang did not know what to make of her story. "I only came to your home today because I heard about your mother," said the woman. "I believe she can be healed."

Sister Zhang invited the woman in and led her to her mother's bed. After a few minutes of friendly conversation, the stranger gently laid her hands on her forehead and began to pray the words of Jesus: "Have faith in God. . . . I tell you the truth, if anyone says to this mountain, 'Go, throw yourself into the sea,' and does not doubt in his heart but believes that what he says will happen, it will be done for him. Therefore I tell you, whatever you ask for in prayer, believe that you have received it, and it will be yours" (Mark 11:22–24).

Sister Zhang would have thought nothing about these words, except that the next afternoon her mother sat up in bed. That day she began walking for the first time in two weeks.

"How does your head feel, Mother?" asked Sister Zhang.

"It feels perfectly fine. The headaches are gone. The pain is gone." Sister Zhang's mother was completely healed. Several weeks later, the woman who had come by to pray returned. Sister Zhang talked about her mother's renewed health. During the conversation, she said to the woman, "Tell me more about this person you call Jesus." For over an hour the woman led Sister Zhang through the Book she had brought with her. For every passage the woman read and tried to explain, Sister Zhang had several more questions.

"Please leave the Book with me so I can read it," Sister Zhang said. The woman paused. She knew that because of Mao Zedong's Cultural Revolution, thousands of Bibles had been burned. She knew that in this region of 20,000 people only a handful of Scriptures existed. Now Sister Zhang wanted to keep one of them.

The woman took the Book from her lap and put it on the table. "I can leave this with you for one week," she said. "Then I will need it back. Someday you will understand."

That night, after the woman left, Sister Zhang did something so natural she thought nothing of it. She took the only piece of paper and pencil she could find and began copying the words of this book called "The New Testament." If she couldn't keep the book, she thought, at least she could find a way to hold on to the words.

All day and all evening Sister Zhang kept writing. For the next several days, while her mother resumed her own regular chores, Sister Zhang hardly cooked or cleaned. By copying the New Testament she had ignored a critical chore. She had failed to collect firewood needed to stoke the fire that warmed their small, thin-walled home. When her angry father confronted her, Sister Zhang apologized. She decided to stop copying the Scriptures. Obeying her father, which the Bible talked about, meant she would only be able to know a fraction of the Book.

The next morning, when Sister Zhang's father went outside, he saw a strange sight: strong winds the night before had sliced off branches of some trees he had never noticed. He filled his arms with loose branches, carried then inside, and fed them into the tiny stove.

Unlike the wood Sister Zhang normally collected, these branches didn't burn for minutes, they burned for hours. He was so delighted he piled up stacks and stacks of the new branches, enough for months of fires. Freed by an act of Providence, Sister Zhang kept copying page after page. As she wrote, she came to the words the woman had prayed: "Because you have so little faith. I tell you the truth, if you have faith as small as a mustard seed, you can say to this mountain, 'Move from here to there' and it will move. Nothing will be impossible for you" (Matt. 17:20).

As Sister Zhang wrote, her parents looked on, curious and amazed. Her father, a staunch Communist official, could not ignore the restored health of his wife and the joy in his daughter. He and his wife began reading the words

Sister Zhang had copied by hand, and all three of them believed.

With the woman's permission, Sister Zhang kept the New Testament a few more days until she had copied all twenty-seven books of the New Testament in her own hand-writing. In the months that followed, she felt a natural desire to share these words. When she spoke, people wanted to hear more. It was clear to the pastors who listened and observed her that Sister Zhang had the gift of preaching.

She began her formal ministry at age thirty-five, going from house church to house church on foot. Often she walked sixty miles to reach the next site. As the number of house churches increased, Sister Zhang had to walk twelve miles each way.

Two thousand years after Peter's first sermon, Sister Zhang was seeing the first church in her midst. In her diary she wrote:

> One woman, eighty-two years old, had been paralyzed for thirty years. At one point in the meeting she stood up and ran forward to give thanks to God. More than thirty people came to the Lord as a result.
>
> A young woman I visited had a severe brain disease. Doctors at the hospital declared her situation hopeless. That night the brothers and sisters prayed for her, and she was healed.
>
> Everywhere I go in China the Holy Spirit is moving. Many people, in numbers I have never seen before, are accepting Christ. At a New Year's meeting of 2,000 pastors and church leaders, one of the brothers saw an image, a vision, of Jesus sitting on the throne. Then there was a voice: "You have to go and win the people, to make them my disciples." In the vision, all the preachers around the throne, all Chinese men and women, went out in all directions to spread the gospel.
>
> The pastors in the room left the meeting knowing God

had spoken to them. They believed God was calling them
to spread out, to take the gospel throughout China and
make disciples. Before they left, they asked all of us at
the meeting to bring new converts. In just one week's
time, one woman brought thirty-five people to Christ. In
two months 47,000 people have given their lives to the
Lord.

This is how spending a few moments in the Bible can
lead to new joy, the joy of a sixteen-year-old girl who saw
God move mountains and who wanted His life and His Book
for herself.

This is how cherishing the Word brings undeniable joy:
Joy that gives a taxi driver and a passenger a new reason
to live, joy that makes time for students whose destinies
are worth more than a lucrative salary, joy that transforms
life in a tiny cell and brings hope and food to prisoners.

This is "the secret of being content," the invisible Christ
being made visible. This is what joy looks like in people
who cherish the Word.

Going Deeper in the Word

Each of the people in this chapter experienced joy
because they approached Scripture as if their lives
depended on it. Whether the Bible is a new acquaintance
or an old friend you'd like to know again, you can deepen
your relationship with God and His Word right now. If you
want to know how writing a few verses can begin to change
you from the inside out, turn the page.

CHAPTER SEVEN

Memorizing the Word

How the Word of Life Can Become Life Itself in You

———∞———

To them God has chosen to make known among the Gentiles the glorious riches of this mystery, which is Christ in you, the hope of glory.

Colossians 1:27

And we know that in all things God works for the good of those who love him, who have been called according to his purpose.

Romans 8:28

"My grace is sufficient for you, for my power is made perfect in weakness."

2 Corinthians 12:9

George Chen stood in front of the small congregation in his native China and said, "This is the day the Lord has made; let us rejoice and be glad in it" (Ps. 118:24). A few feet outside the main entrance of the house in which the people gathered, three Communist party authorities armed with guns waited to arrest him.

For spreading the gospel, for being convicted of treason, George Chen spent the next eighteen years in prison. For nearly two decades he did not see a single copy of the Bible. For seven of those years he worked ten hours a day in one of the most wretched, offensive settings imaginable.

Yet it was this very experience that caused George to sing hymns at the top of his lungs. Guards and fellow inmates could not comprehend his happiness. They could not grasp the truth that would allow George to survive.

By memorizing portions of the Word, George not only embraced the Word as a trusted guide for daily living, he experienced the Word as life *itself*.

Here is the unusual, little-known story of what took place, the story that George Chen tells in his own words.

Songs of Comfort . . . and Sorrow

"In the early 1930s, Shanghai was the most modern city in China, a growing vacation and investment center for Asia. For thousands of other Chinese like myself, however, Shanghai was a bitter memory.

"Our family of six shared a one-room flat in the city. Every morning I woke up to the smell of coal smoke from the kitchen stove that had burned all night. Our house had no toilet and no piped-in water. Everyone in the building had to use an outside public faucet; but we always had food to eat, including rice and vegetables, and, if we were lucky, a little chicken or beef.

"Within a few years the scenery shifted. My father's business decisions paid off and we moved into a large, four-room house with a living and dining room, plumbing, and two toilets. My mother cooked with a gas stove. When she wasn't fixing meals, she took care of every pair of socks, every piece of clothing, everything my siblings and I needed. Since my father was often gone, my mother was the one who cared for us. She chose the good schools and checked our lessons every day. She made our family run.

"Then, when I was thirteen, she became very ill and entered the hospital. When she came back home she was better, and she was not the same person. The first morning after she got out of bed, she collected all of the Buddha statues in our living room and threw them in the garbage.

"'What are you doing, Mother? What's gotten into you?' I asked as she methodically stripped the walls of thousands of years of Chinese culture and our religious identity.

"My mother didn't care because for the first time in her life she was happy. While she was in the hospital someone had given her a book about another religion and its leader, Jesus Christ. She had begun reading the eyewitness accounts of His life, His execution, and His resurrection.

"She showed us the book she'd been given and admonished us to read it. At first the book didn't seem that much different from Buddhism, since both talked about doing good works. Nevertheless, I read the Bible because my mother couldn't quit talking about it.

"Right before Christmas, my siblings and I were getting ready to fly with our father on a plane to Hong Kong. I remember mother taking us to the airport in Shanghai. Her belief in Jesus Christ and the book that contained His story had grown stronger. As we waited to board the plane, she began to sing to us in the airport lobby:

> 'God be with you till we meet again,
> By His counsels guide, uphold you,
> With His sheep securely fold you;
> God be with you till we meet again.'

"My siblings and I listened, bundled in thick coats ready to board the plane. My mother straightened our collars and checked to make sure we had our tickets. Then, one by one, she hugged us. I could feel her arms around me as she pressed her warm cheeks against mine. Then she stepped back, looked at the four of us, and sang:

> 'Till we meet, till we meet,
> Till we meet at Jesus' feet,
> God be with you till we meet again.'

"As we turned to board the plane I looked back and saw my mother smiling and waving. It was the last time I would ever see her.

"A few days after arriving in Hong Kong, my father, brothers, sister, and I waited at the airport for my mother's flight to arrive. After several hours the officials told us to leave; they said the airport was closed. The next morning my father handed me the newspaper. The plane carrying my mother and at least a hundred other passengers had crashed off a small island near Hong Kong.

"A day didn't go by when I didn't miss her. Every time I closed my eyes I saw her bright face and heard her singing, 'We will meet each other, again, when we meet at Jesus' feet.'

"*Could this really be true?* I thought. *Could Jesus be right when He said, 'I am the way and the truth and the life'[John 14:16]? Is He the God who created everything? Is He really the Savior?* With these questions tumbling around inside, I began to read the Bible, and as I read, my heart opened up. I felt like God was speaking about me. It was a special feeling, one I couldn't describe. Eventually I could not deny what I felt and believed inside, that Jesus was God and that I belonged to Him.

The Curtain Falls

"In that year, 1951, another kind of change was taking place—throughout China. Two years earlier, the Chinese Communist Party had begun its methodical, brutal take-over of the country.

"When the Communists came to power in China they said nothing would change; everything would remain the same. They encouraged capitalists to keep their businesses. The Communists told landowners their property would be protected. In rural areas they even gave land to farmers.

"The Communists never kept their promise. Once the government seized all land and all income, farmers had no sense of ownership and no motivation to produce.

"While 'land reform' turned into an economic and agricultural disaster, our life in Shanghai remained stable until mass political movements began, and the Communists began to show their true colors. They despised anyone who earned a decent living. If you made money, like my father, you were looked down upon and ridiculed.

"The Communists brainwashed my father's employees and pressured them to spread lies about him. Through economic restrictions, taxes, and deceit they drained him of his money and his spirit. Through endless harassment they forced him to make false confessions that he had stolen from the government.

Threatened Yet Unbowed

"Though I was concerned, I did not worry. I understood that God was in control of everything that happened. The reason I was so sure was that I had a Bible. I read it fervently. Through the Bible I could approach God personally and directly at any time, night or day. Regardless of where I was or what I was feeling, the Bible was a constant reminder of God's truth and His love for me.

"The more I read the Lord's Word, the more I realized God cared about China's people. As I assisted a house-church pastor and learned to care for others, I knew God was calling me to be an evangelist. I knew the Communists were monitoring pastors and pressuring them to stop preaching, but their threats did nothing to deter me from the work I knew God wanted me to do.

"My biggest concern had always been for the people in China's remote villages. As a child, I had visited this countryside of beautiful mountains, lakes, and trees. Not until I served there as a pastor, not until I went to live in a remote seacoast village, did I realize how hard their life could be.

Only a Matter of Time

"On the coast of northern China I learned the meaning of the word *poor* from people whose survival depended on harvesting salt from the ocean. After intentionally flooding their fields, they scraped acres of white, sun-dried earth into huge mounds so the salt's essence could drip into hundreds of small jars. For this tedious, backbreaking routine the people earned next to nothing.

"Before I arrived in the village, few, if any, of the people had even heard of Christianity. Almost no one had seen a Bible. Yet, as the villagers got to know me, they trusted me. They opened their doors and invited me in. They were eager to hear and learn about the Christian God and the book I had brought them.

"The villagers found the Bible fascinating. They read it, they asked questions, and, one by one, they came to believe in God and in His Book. A handful of new believers grew to three hundred. Considering the constant threat of harassment and persecution by the Communists, such an increase was astounding—especially when scores of pastors were being led out of services, pulled out of homes, and taken off to jail. My time came several months later, in 1954.

"I was working in the village when officials approached me one day and led me to jail. To them I was a stranger, a spy from another country. None of my explanations did any good. I spent the next month in a cell with a handful of others, but I wasn't worried or afraid. Even though I lost my freedom for thirty days, I knew God was with me. Upon my release one official told me, 'You will return to Shanghai to get a permit. Otherwise, you cannot continue your work as a pastor.'

"From that day on I knew the Communists were always watching me. When I traveled to Shanghai or made my way back to the sea village, I knew every move was being monitored and recorded. Again, two years later, I found myself in prison. Again I was released, this time after two months.

The Need for Cell Groups

"Then, in 1958, life in China changed forever with the formal coming to power of Mao Zedong. The brutal political upheaval he caused, and its reverberations on the church in China, have been well-documented:

"In 1949 there were around two hundred Three-Self churches in buildings registered with the government. 'Underground' house churches, to which I gave my allegiance, were too numerous to count. After the Communist revolution in 1949, the government churches seemed unchanged.

"But from 1954 to 1957 that facade crumbled. The next reform movement, called socialism, reduced the church to eight congregations in Shanghai alone. In Beijing, sixty-six churches dwindled to only four. Those not under government control closed, and even those that survived were merged with smaller churches. In all of China, just one Bible seminary remained.

"We house church pastors—and there had to be thousands of us—knew we were living on borrowed time. Eventually, we knew we would go to prison for weeks, perhaps for months. None of us, including myself, thought we would spend nearly two decades in prison.

"My final arrest came in 1960. The Communists called me a counterrevolutionary and accused me of concealing my activities within my Christian beliefs. I was sentenced to prison, with little or no possibility of release.

"The Waterloo Bridge Prison in Shanghai had many buildings and hundreds of cells like mine, six feet long and

five feet wide. Laying down lengthwise, I could have
reached out my arms and touched both sides at once. I
never had that chance, however, because I shared the cell
with four other prisoners. It was so cramped that at night
we had to sleep head to toe.

"The cell had no toilet, just a wooden stool that was used
and reused many times a day, hosed off by the guards and
then returned to us. Because there was so little space, one
person had to lay his head next to the stool each night.
Sometimes during the day urine would run out underneath
the iron gate, the only open space where light was allowed
to enter.

"Each day we woke up at six o'clock to the shrill blast of
a guard's whistle. Breakfast was a small bowl of watery
rice soup. Lunch and dinner were a repeat of breakfast.
The highlight of the day came in the afternoon when I had
twenty minutes to walk around the yard. After the whistle
sounded, I spent the rest of the day back inside my five-by-
six-foot cubicle.

Hidden in the Heart

"Days blurred into weeks and dissolved into months.
Though I felt the seasons change, I lost track of the years.
One thing kept me alive, and that was the thought of my
friends in the sea village. Most had received only two years
of schooling, so they didn't know how to read or write. The
only way they had been able to learn the Bible was by my
reading passages to them out loud. They repeated the
verses and told them to each other until they had memorized the words. Though they couldn't read a single word,
they learned the Word of God by heart. Though totally illit-
erate, they had taught me how God's Word could live inside
me—through memorization.

"In the cell I was forbidden to say any verses out loud, so
I spoke them to myself. Every night I recited to myself the

words of 2 Corinthians 12:9: 'My grace is sufficient for you, for my power is made perfect in weakness.' Strangely and wonderfully, by memorizing the Bible, by meditating on His Word in silence, I could hear God speaking to me.

"And how I needed Him. After four years in prison I had lost more than fifty pounds, nearly a third of my total body weight. Severe indigestion was as constant as breathing. Nothing, I thought, could be worse than the grim food, the dark cell, the sense of hopelessness I woke up to each morning. I was wrong.

"For reasons I'll never know, I was transferred by boat to a labor camp outside of Shanghai. Once inside the compound, I was thrown into a brigade of two to four thousand prisoners ordered to farm hundreds of acres. Our days began before dawn and ended at dusk. For twelve to fourteen hours a day I stood knee-deep in rice fields, hoeing and planting while fighting off deadly mosquitoes.

"Again I thought back to the people in the sea village. Every day I praised my Lord because I could recite the Scriptures. Every time I recited the Twenty-third Psalm, I could feel the Lord with me. Never once did I feel depressed or sad.

"Then, one morning in 1964, a prison official scowled at me and said, 'Your time of working in the fields is over. From now on, you have a new job.' He then led me to an area of the labor camp no one ever talked about, a place no one wanted to go near.

"As we walked to the site I saw hatred in the face of the prison guards; they despised me because I was a Christian who didn't believe in their system, and for that they decided to exact their revenge.

"Before I even saw my work site for the next five years, I could smell it from a distance. The guard led me to a field of human waste. It was the cesspool for the entire prison. The stench was overwhelming, and at first it choked my breathing. Not only was the aroma repulsive, the excrement contained poisonous viruses that could kill.

"The guard ordered me to pick up a shovel. Then he briefly explained my new job. Though I couldn't believe what he was telling me to do, I had no choice but to obey him that day and all the days that followed.

"Every morning before the sun came up, I put on my only pair of short pants and my T-shirt and walked forty minutes down a narrow dirt road to the human waste cesspool. It was six feet wide, six feet long, and more than six feet deep. My job was to dig out all the contents into a pile where it would be made into fertilizer.

"The problem with the pit was that I couldn't stand on the edge, bend down, and scoop out the waste. The only way I could dig it out was to actually stand in the pit. With no boots to wear, with just a pair of socks I coated every morning with water-resistant oil, with no gloves, and with nothing to cover my mouth, I shoveled human waste for eight to ten hours a day.

"At first I didn't know if I would survive, or even make it through the day. I figured it was only a matter of time before the bacteria and mosquitoes made me ill. All the previous warnings, harassments, and arrests, even the crowded, miserable cell I had lived in for five years, seemed inviting compared to this.

"One thing was unusual about the cesspool. In the farm field I had been one of several thousand prisoners under the watchful eyes of the guards. Now, because of the terrible stench, no prisoners or guards dared to come near me. For ten hours a day I saw no one, I heard no one, I talked to no one.

Alone with God

"The loneliness and frustration welled up inside me. Feelings would come to the surface, feelings I could no longer keep inside:

'Lord, give me the strength to dig out this pit!'

'Lord, this seems like too much.'

'Lord, I need strength, *Your* strength. I need Your peace that's beyond my own understanding.'

"Never before in prison had I been able to hear my own voice out loud. In my cries to the Lord, I realized that the isolation of the human waste cesspool had brought me unexpected blessing. For the first time in years I was all alone, alone with God, and by being alone with God I was suddenly free! In the cesspool I was free to speak, free to pray, free to worship my Lord out loud. The cesspool, the place no one else dared to come near, became my refuge, my quiet refuge, my personal sanctuary with my Lord.

"In the cesspool I felt God's blessing every day. Every day I dug out the same pit that had been filled up the night before. As I worked, I recited the words I had memorized: 'And we know that in all things God works for the good of those who love him, who have been called according to his purpose' (Rom. 8:28).

"By carrying these words in my heart, God's Word filled my heart and gave me new life, but perhaps the deepest experience of His Word in me came through a hymn. I had sung it many times at the church back in Shanghai. Like Scripture, I had memorized the lyrics, so when the melody came to my mind, the words flowed:

> 'I come to the garden alone
> While the dew is still on the roses.
> And the voice I hear falling on my ear,
> The Son of God discloses.
> And He walks with me and He talks with me
> And He tells me I am His own.
> And the joy we share as we tarry there
> No other has ever known.
> I'd stay in the garden with Him
> Though the night around me be falling.

But He bids me go through the voice of woe
His voice to me is calling.'

"For some reason I liked this hymn. It touched something inside me, something I could not quite explain. Each time I sang it, the melody and the words spoke to me louder and louder:

'He speaks and the sound of His voice
Is so sweet the birds hush their singing.
And the melody that He gave to me
Within my heart is ringing.'

"While I sang this hymn I never stopped working. I stood in the pit with my hands on the shovel and my mouth open. Soon, it was more than a song, it was my prayer to God:

'I come to the garden alone
While the dew is still on the roses.
And the voice I hear falling on my ear,
The Son of God discloses.'

"As I sang, a strange thing happened: I did not smell the stench. With every word, all I became aware of, all that mattered to me, was my Lord:

'And He walks with me and He talks with me
And He tells me I am His own.
And the joy we share as we tarry there
No other has ever known.'

"Suddenly I understood why God had given me this wonderful hymn. In His Word the Lord promised He would never leave me nor forsake me. In the cesspool I was alone with my Lord, to walk with Him and to talk to Him.

"At that moment it became clear: the human waste cesspool was my garden! It was the place God had reserved for Him and me. The Communists thought they were punishing me. They didn't realize what they had done to bless me!

Every day I worked in the cesspool was a day to sing because God was in the song, and the song was in my heart to stay.

"I'll never know exactly why the prison guards came to me one day and told me it was time to leave the cesspool and return to the farm fields. Maybe they thought that five years of doing the same job was enough for one person. They didn't know how God had met me. They also didn't know the sorrows I carried inside.

Memory's Gift

"After ten years in prison, I received a letter from my wife. Since 1960 she had waited for my release. Now she said she could wait no longer. She was getting a divorce and keeping my only child. For years I knew I had at least two people waiting for me on the outside. Now I truly had no one to count on but the Lord. Even this most precious relationship seemed to be in danger.

"I hadn't held a Bible in my hands in over ten years. Without being able to read the actual words, precious passages I thought I'd never lose began to fade from my mind.

"I was not alone. Thousands of other imprisoned pastors throughout China grieved too. They grieved for not being able to hold and read the Scriptures. They grieved for their churches when new, incoming prisoners relayed the news of Mao Zedong's Cultural Revolution sweeping across China, of millions being pushed aside and murdered all in the name of Communism.

"Religion was Mao's number one target. All churches were declared illegal. All Christian activities were banned. When I heard how Bibles by the thousands were being collected and burned, I wept. I thought of the first villagers I had served. I pictured Christians in the sea village not being able to worship, sing, and read the Scriptures. My deepest sorrow was not knowing for sure if they were alive or dead.

"As the months in prison dragged on, more and more verses faded from my memory. Yet, because I had memorized the Word, I could still hear the Lord speaking: "My grace is sufficient for you, for my power is made perfect in weakness" (2 Cor. 12:91). I was holding on to these words in 1976 when I learned that Mao Zedong had died.

Freedom

The power struggle that followed shook every national institution in China. Prison doors opened and I was freed. No explanation was given. I remember seeing the faces of Christian friends waiting for me outside the prison gates. I remember one of them laying a Bible in my hands. For the first time in eighteen years I turned the pages and saw the words from the Song of Solomon I had barely remembered: "All night long on my bed I looked for the one my heart loves; I looked for him but did not find him. I will get up now and go about the city, through its streets and squares; I will search for the one my heart loves (3:1–2).

One Momentous Homecoming

In these words I knew what I had to do. I had to get up and search for the ones my heart loved. I had to go back to the seacoast village. I had to find my brothers and sisters who had been my life, and for whom the Word meant life itself.

The journey to the seacoast was an eight-hour train ride, followed by a three-hour walk and a one-and-a-half-hour bus ride. After a one-and-a-half hour bicycle ride to the edge of town, the village I hadn't seen in nearly two decades came into view. The land was still desolate, white with ocean salt. Only a few, small, tile-roofed houses dotted the shore.

I made my way into the village and found the house where I was told the Christians were waiting to meet me. When I saw the bicycles outside, my heart started to beat faster. I didn't know what to expect. I didn't know who or what I would find.

The front of the house was bare. Though there were no signs of people, I came in through the front door. The house was totally still. I wanted to sit down and rest, but a greeter at the door wouldn't let me.

"They are outside in the back," he said, "and they're waiting to meet you." I followed him out through a dark passageway, wondering all along what I would see on the other side. A few more seconds, a few more steps, and the back door swung open.

Suddenly I saw a courtyard filled with people. Not twenty, or fifty, but hundreds of them, all standing in silence. There were women and men of all ages, elderly gentlemen and young mothers. There were children, teenagers, and toddlers who had not yet been born when I went to prison. While I stood there they said nothing. They simply looked at me in silence.

I was dumbfounded and speechless. How could there be so many Christians? How, when all of China's pastors had been in prison for the past twenty years? When I was led away by guards in 1960 there were only three hundred believers in the village. Now, I was told, there were five thousand Christians meeting in twenty different house churches!

"How can this be possible?" I asked one of the leaders standing next to me. "All these years you had no pastors and few, if any, Bibles. You've been under severe persecution all along. How could the church have possibly grown?"

"The Lord was working the whole time," he said. "The Holy Spirit worked in the hearts of people, and look what has happened!" Indeed, the evidence was right before my eyes.

"All things work together for good to them that love Thee, O Lord!" I said loudly. Then I addressed the people. I began to share some of the things I had learned about God while I had been away from them in prison.

During the next few days, it was my chance to learn about them. I was surprised to find out that the church no longer held three-hour services, divided equally between singing and preaching. Now, wherever I went, I was asked to preach for five hours at a time! I was both blessed and yet still puzzled. "How did the church grow to be so strong?" I asked.

"When the Communists banned all religious activities," they replied, "we were left with no leaders. There was no pastor to teach us, no evangelist to instruct us. The only way to seek God's revelation and truth was to ask the Holy Spirit to move in us and to learn from the few Bibles we had."

It was obvious that for the past two decades God had answered the prayers of His people in China. God knew what thousands of pastors like myself did not know at the time. Twenty years earlier, none of us had known how to teach, lead, or guide new believers. Had China's pastors been free to speak, we would have tried to arrange everything for the people, and then the people would have been tempted to look to other human beings for direction and strength. But because leaders were absent, the people had to look to God and to His Word.

As a church, China's Christians learned what I had discovered in my garden: When everything we've come to depend upon is gone—when situations worsen and hope fades—the only things no one can take away are our faith and the portions of God's Word that live inside us.

Had I not memorized the Word, I would not have been able to call upon the Lord when I needed Him most.

Without memorizing the Word when it was available to me, I would have missed out on what I needed to survive—the Word that brings life, *and becomes life itself.*

Goıng Deeper ın The Word

You can begin to take the Word to heart today. By investing a few minutes each day, your faith, your love for God and His Word, can keep growing for a lifetime. An excellent place to explore this new possibility is on page 133 in chapter 9, "Twenty-Eight Days That Can Change Your Life."

One warning: If you commit yourself to Scripture memory, you'll commit yourself to a new way of living. You may find yourself facing risks and sacrifices you never imagined. Then you'll understand what made a person like Doug Nichols tick, especially as he acted on the Word and discovered, for himself, the advantages of having cancer.

CHAPTER EIGHT

Acting on the Word

How Living the Bible Can Make All the Difference

———∞———

> You have made known to me the path of life; you will fill me with joy in your presence, with eternal pleasures at your right hand.
>
> Psalm 16:11

Doug Nichols wiped the sweat from his forehead. His heart pounded as he stood on the porch of the farmhouse he remembered some forty years ago in this desert of southern California's Coachella Valley. He had dreaded this moment. Once he knocked on the screen door he knew it was too late. He knew he couldn't back out.

The next few seconds felt like years. A thin, gray-haired woman came to the door. In her arms was a baby.

"Can I help you?" she asked.

Behind her, Doug could see an empty living room and bare floors. He swallowed hard and tried to speak.

"Ma'am, have you lived in this house for long?"

"Yes, many years," she replied.

"Did you ever rent your land to some boys in high school to raise cattle?"

"Yes."

"I was one of those boys," said Doug. He bounced the palms of his hands against his pant legs, and then looked down and back up until his eyes met hers.

"Ma'am, I never paid you. I cheated you out of money you should have received."

The woman tried to make sense of the young stranger and what he was telling her. "It's been so long I don't really remember the exact dates or the money," she said.

"All I have to my name is thirty dollars," said Doug. As he reached out to hand her the wad of crumpled bills, the woman began to cry.

"My husband and I are totally broke. Right now he's downtown standing on a street corner begging for money so we can buy food to eat tonight." She dried her eyes while repeating the words, "Thank you." Then she asked Doug, "Why did you do this?"

"It is just something I should do."

Late one night, after staggering up the stairs of his dormitory, Doug Nichols began telling a friend why he was so directionless and unhappy. By the time the sun came up, Doug was praying to give his life to Jesus Christ.

Days later, as he was reading the Bible, he came to a verse in Romans that stopped him cold: "Owe no man any thing" (Rom. 13:8). "Once I read those words I had to act," he said. "There was no other way to live."

This conviction sums up what makes an ordinary person like Doug Nichols such a practical example of how following the Bible can make all the difference in a person's life.

Instead of ignoring what he knew God was telling him to do, Doug Nichols acted on the Word. Since that pivotal day on the farmhouse porch, acting on the Word has become a freeing way of life for Doug. Three times when his faith was at a crossroads, Doug was totally honest with himself and God:

"Lord, I don't know how to obey You."

"Lord, I don't know if I can trust You."

"Lord, I'm not sure I have what it takes to believe in You."

Each time he prayed to the Lord, Doug seriously considered what it meant to follow God's Word. Each time his responses, guided by the Scriptures, surprised, confused, and even angered onlookers. For Doug Nichols, acting on the Word out of a deepening love for God has made all the difference. The beauty of it all is that he could let his actions speak for themselves.

Three weeks after Doug Nichols arrived as a twenty-one-year-old freshman at Prairie Bible Institute in Canada he was flunking all his classes. One Saturday morning he sat on the edge of his bed and cried, "Lord, I feel like such a failure. I want to serve you, but I don't know how. I feel I've wasted my life."

At that moment he heard a knock at his door, and a man walked in the room. The visitor was Norman Charter, a retired missionary who worked at the school.

"Doug, I know you didn't call or ask me to come by, but I've been praying for you. I know you've been going through a hard time with your studies. This morning after I went over the records of new freshmen, including yours, I put on my overcoat and walked across campus in the direction of your dorm. I felt the Lord wanted me to see you."

"I need to leave school, sir. I know I love God, but it's obvious I don't have what it takes to make it as a student," Doug said.

Norman Charter listened and then calmly replied, "Didn't you come here to study the Word of God? What good will it do for you to leave?"

Doug was silent. With nowhere else to turn and his grades at rock bottom, Doug Nichols decided to stay in school. He entered a tutoring program. For the next three years he studied constantly, and by the time he completed his coursework, he had made A's in two classes.

But after graduation came more discouragement. Doug applied to twenty mission organizations and was rejected by all twenty. Only one other group, Operation Mobilization, said yes.

After two years in India, Doug and his wife, Margaret, were helping senior missionaries start new churches in the Philippines when adversity struck again. Illness forced the ministry's director to leave suddenly, and within days the board named Doug the new director of Christ for Greater Manila. He was overwhelmed. How could he follow God's Word and "preach good news to the poor" (Luke 4:18) in a city of six million people, many of whom had given up hope for a better life?

Doug found himself asking this question one morning as he stood next to a Filipino coworker named Aires on the huge garbage dump in Manila known as Smoky Mountain. As the sun came up over the infamous refuse site fifteen thousand squatters called home, Doug prayed, "God, help us and the other team members to effectively reach these very poor and needy people with the good news of salvation in Christ."

The words were barely out of his mouth when a man approached them. He wore tattered shorts and carried a dirty burlap bag. He told them he had started scavenging aluminum cans even though he was so weak he could carry only a few cans in his bag at a time. The man asked Doug if he would guard his few cans while he continued his work. Doug agreed.

As the man came and went with his tin cans, Doug and Aires talked about evangelism and discipleship. Not thinking about the man, they continued praying: "Lord, you have commanded us to take the gospel to all, including the people at this garbage dump. Give us wisdom to know how to reach them."

When the man walked back with another small load of cans, Doug could see he was quite elderly. Doug knew that in parts of Asia, especially in the Philippines, it was respectful to ask older people their age. "How wonderful that you asked," said the man. "Today is my birthday. I'm seventy-eight years old."

Doug and Aires offered their congratulations with a chorus of "Happy Birthday." When they hugged the stranger, he kept saying, "Thanks!" Then, in a very easy manner, Doug asked him, "Are you prepared to go to heaven?" The man didn't know how to respond because he had never heard of heaven.

Over the next few minutes, as Doug and Aires talked, the man with the burlap sack heard the story of Jesus for the first time in his seventy-eight years. After he had listened closely to the two young men, he said, "I want to accept Christ as my Savior."

After Doug and Aires made their way back down the garbage heap, the man invited them into a small, dark shack to meet his son, daughter-in-law, and grandchildren. There he told his family he was prepared to follow Christ for the rest of his life.

Results of Obedience

Doug Nichols had stood at a crossroads of faith. Instead of letting himself be paralyzed by indecision or doubt, he acted on faith. By praying a few words from Scripture, Doug Nichols acted on the Word. As a result, the daunting task of taking the gospel to Manila's six million people became a little less daunting because Doug and a friend had brought the promise of heaven to one person.

By his actions Doug Nichols said, "I will obey You, Lord." By following the Word, Doug Nichols saw God's promises on the printed page come to life and change *his* life, and God provided avenues to reach the downtrodden of the Philippines:

- With their team, the Nichols started a ministry to prisoners and prostitutes.
- They expanded a camping ministry to street children and created a "Home of Joy" to care for abandoned children in Manila.
- They opened a rescue home where troubled street youth could find a new way to live free from harmful addictions.
- Doug Nichols—a man who had never seen himself as a leader—trained and directed over 175 short-term missionaries and 250 Filipino workers.
- Over the next twenty years, the tiny ministry Doug once felt too inadequate to manage grew into Action International Ministries (ACTION), with 127 short-term missionaries serving in nine countries.

A 30 Percent Chance to Live

A few years later, when Nichols had resettled near Seattle, God's Word hit home with new urgency. One day, after a routine physical checkup, Doug's doctor phoned saying, "I need to see you right now." Twenty minutes later, Doug heard the news in person: "You have colon cancer. You need to have surgery immediately. You may even need to have a colostomy, a hole in your side where a bag attaches." Then the doctor explained how far he believed the cancer had spread.

Doug listened, and then stood up and started for the door. "Sit down!" said the doctor. "Don't you understand how serious this is?"

Doug stopped. As his patient turned around, the doctor could see the tears in Doug's eyes. "What you just told me is terrible," said Doug. "I'm scared to death. Even so, I'll share something with you. I'm a Christian. I'm a follower of God and the Lord Jesus Christ. If God can't help me right now, I couldn't trust Him for anything, could I?"

The doctor paused, then said, "You're right."

"If it's OK with you," said Doug, "I'm going to trust God through this whole thing." By now the cancer had spread through the wall of Doug's intestines and into the surrounding lymph nodes. The doctor gave Doug only a 30 percent chance to live one more year.

After surgery, with the colostomy a disquieting fact of life, Doug went through months of torturous radiation and chemotherapy. Remarkably, he felt at peace. Numerous friends told Doug they believed God had allowed him to have cancer for some greater, unrevealed purpose. "I don't believe God allowed me to have cancer," Doug replied. "I believe He gave me cancer."

"How can you be so sure of God's love when you're facing such a terrible disease?" they asked.

"I believe God is good to me because I trust His Word. It's only because of the Word that I came to know Christ. It's only because of the Word I began to live a new life repaying the people I had robbed. It's only because of the Word, and living my life on the basis of what God calls us to do, that I believe my cancer can be used for His purposes. I can say these things to you because I believe the psalmist's words are true: 'Praise our God, O peoples, let the sound of his praise be heard; he has preserved our lives and kept our feet from slipping. For you, O God, tested us; you refined us like silver. You brought us into prison and laid burdens on our backs'" (Ps. 66:8–11).

Throughout the long months of treatment, Doug's pain and discomfort grew. When he wanted to give up, when he thought it was all too much to go through, Margaret related to Doug the completion of the psalmist's promise: "'You let men ride over our heads; we went through fire and water, but you brought us to a place of abundance'" (Ps. 66:12).

Doug then responded by praying, "Lord, I'm hurting. All I know how to do is trust You. All that I have and all that I am I entrust to You."

At a second crossroads of faith, Doug realized that *obeying* the Word had prepared him to *trust* the Word.

Neither Doug nor Margaret could know that God was preparing them to face a third, and most remarkable, crossroads of faith, one that the psalmist had already described: "You have made known to me the path of life; you will fill me with joy in your presence, with eternal pleasures at your right hand" (Ps. 16:11).

"You Can't Go to Rwanda!"

It happened in August 1994. One night after dinner, Doug and Margaret watched the television news reports of millions of frightened refugees fleeing the genocide of Rwanda's senseless civil war.

That night the psalmist's promised "path of life" became a troubled road filled with starving, deserted babies who had nowhere to go. As Doug saw their faces he said to himself, "This is not right. As a Christian, I could act. As a Christian, I've got to act."

That week, Doug and a small team ran ACTION's faxed pleas to Christian organizations, asking for people to help them meet the crisis in Rwanda. Sixteen men and women, including physicians, nurses, and medical technicians, responded and volunteered to go with Doug to Africa.

There was just one snag.

A year of radiation and excessive chemotherapy had destroyed Doug's immune system. When he announced his travel plans to his doctor, the oncologist said, "You can't go to Rwanda. Your body is so weak you'll die in three days from cholera, dysentery, or meningitis. To be honest, I can't believe you're even thinking of going. For over a year I've worked to keep you alive, and you want to risk it all just to hold a few dying babies."

Doug looked at his doctor and said, "Being Jewish, you may remember the Old Testament story of Esther. When

Mordecai, Esther's uncle, looked at Esther, he wondered aloud, 'And who knows but that you have come to royal position for such a time as this?' [Esther 4:14]. Do you think God could possibly be using you to keep me alive for such a time as this, for such a time as Rwanda?"

The doctor was nonplussed. He knew nothing he could say or do would keep Doug from going.

That night, before he left for Africa, Doug knelt by the side of his bed and prayed: "Lord, I know the path of life You've made known to me. I know it's a path that will lead me to children who are dying of cholera and AIDS. I know that by caring for them I could die. Even so I will still go. If I can hold one dying baby for an hour and give it comfort and love, then Your work in this old body of mine will not have been in vain."

At the airport the next day, Margaret couldn't hold back her tears. Though she didn't want Doug to go to Africa just to die, she believed there was a reason he needed to make the trip.

In Rwanda, Doug did exactly what he had planned to do. He walked into a bare cement room filled with thirty-five children. They sat sprawled out on the floor, hungry and crying, their stomachs bloated by sickness. Their parents were either dead or missing. Every child was naked, cold, and wet. In the next several hours Doug tried to hold and comfort as many children as he could, and when he had no more of himself to give he slumped to his knees and cried like one of them.

For the next two weeks, Doug dived into a sea of human misery. Knowing that many Rwandans faced death each day, he did anything he could to help doctors, nurses, and medics reach the sick and traumatized refugees. After ten days, surrounded by coughing, polluted water, and the smell of death, Doug Nichols, the cancer patient with the fragile immune system, was still on his feet. After nearly two weeks of round-the-clock activity, he was one of a few of the entire sixteen team members who had not become sick!

"I'm Not Dead Yet!"

One frenzied afternoon during a break, Doug borrowed a cellular phone and phoned the front desk at the tumor institute in Seattle, where he received his cancer treatments. When the head nurse answered, Doug said, "Alice, I just wanted to phone and let you know . . . I'm not dead yet!"

A few days later, Doug stepped off the elevator at the tumor institute, where nurses hugged him. Behind their smiles they feared he was now infected with one or more life-threatening diseases.

The lab results did not lie. The day after many exhaustive tests, the oncologist who had warned Doug not to go to Rwanda called him into his office. "Your tests come up with what we call 'NED.'"

"What does that stand for?" Doug asked.

"NED is short for 'no evidence of disease.' There is no sign of cancer in your body. I guess Rwanda was good to you. Though it could come back at anytime, the cancer is gone."

Doug smiled and thought of the psalmist's words, which had become his own: "You have made known to me the path of life; you will fill me with joy in your presence, with eternal pleasures at your right hand" (Ps. 16:11).

For Doug Nichols, acting on the Word had made all the difference. Through years of learning to obey God, Doug had come to trust the Word; and by trusting the Word he could say with confidence, "I believe in You, Lord." Doug Nichols had come full circle to a truth he had discovered years ago on a farmhouse porch: True faith in God and in His Word ultimately leads to action.

Saying it is so simple. Living it seems so hard. How does one actually begin to live the Word when it's been silent in our lives longer than we care to admit?

Years ago, as a young missionary in India, Doug Nichols may have answered this question without realizing it. On one of the worst nights of his life, he made the liberating discovery that acting on the Word, the very thing most people find so difficult to do, begins with one, small, hesitant step. This life-changing discovery is at the heart of the story only Doug Nichols can tell.

Cry of a Helpless Man

"In 1967 I went to New Delhi to serve with Operation Mobilization, the only missions group that would accept me. A few months after I arrived, I contracted tuberculosis, but my troubles had just begun. Indian officials refused to admit me to the government free sanitarium. To them I was a rich American. They didn't know that, as a missionary, I was just as broke as they were.

"Once admitted, I soon felt discouraged. The Indian workers and patients didn't like me; I didn't speak their language, and they didn't speak mine. When I tried to hand them a Gospel of John to read, they refused. The silence between us lingered, and so did my sickness.

"After falling asleep I'd wake up early in the morning coughing. One time was particularly bad. In the midst of my hacking, I looked across the room and noticed one of the older, sicker patients trying to get out of bed.

"After minutes of struggling he finally sat up. However, when he tried to move his weight forward, he fell back onto the mattress. He didn't know how weak he really was. Again he strained to sit up. Again he collapsed back onto the sheets. After several tries, he simply gave up. Then, with his head on his pillow, he began to cry softly.

"It wasn't until the next morning that I realized what he'd been trying to do. His sickness had made him so weak he wasn't able to walk to the bathroom. There were no nurses' aides who would help him, no bedpans he could use. Curled up under his covers, this frail man sobbed because he knew he couldn't help himself.

"That morning the smell in our ward was awful. The patients yelled insults at the man. The nurses were agitated at having to clean up the mess. One who moved him roughly from side to side was so angry she slapped him. Feeling embarrassed and ashamed, the man hid his face and wept. As I fell asleep that night I wondered how long this could go on. What could I do but watch?

"Hours later, I woke up coughing. For several minutes I sat up in bed. I felt lousy. Then I looked across the aisle and saw the elderly man. Again he was trying to sit up and go to the washroom. Again he strained to sit up. Again he fell back in bed. Again he cried.

"I hated what I saw. Yet I sure didn't want to become involved. I was sick myself. Then, for some reason, I remembered the words of James 4:17, 'Anyone, then, who knows the good he ought to do and doesn't do it, sins.' Suddenly, before I realized what I was doing, I got out of bed and walked over to the elderly man. By now he was so consumed with his own emotions he didn't know I was next to him.

"I reached down and touched his shoulder. He turned, opened his eyes, and gave me a look of fear. I simply smiled, put one arm under his head and neck, the other arm under his legs, and picked him up.

"Even though I was sick and weak, I could carry him. Tuberculosis and old age had eaten away at his now thin, withered frame. I carried him down the hall to the washroom. Then I stood behind him with my arms under his, holding him up so he could take care of himself. After he finished, I picked him up and carried him back to his bed.

As I began to lay him down, while my head was next to his, he kissed me on the cheek. Then he smiled and said, 'Thank you.'

"What happened the next morning was amazing. One of the other patients who had seen everything got out of bed and woke me around four o'clock with a steaming cup of delicious Indian tea. He knew no English, but motioned with his hands that he wanted one of the small booklets of Scripture. As the sun came up, some of the other patients began to approach me. They, too, gestured that they wanted one of the booklets I had tried to give them.

"Throughout the day, nurses, hospital interns, and doctors came to me asking for gospel booklets until every person in the hospital had a Scripture booklet or Gospel of John. Over the next few days, several of them trusted Jesus Christ as their Savior as a result of reading the good news."

How disarmingly simple: to get up from where you are and care for someone else. How basic: to obey, to trust, to believe, and then to act; to know that the Word you've been reading for years is true because you're living it; and to know that it can all begin with one, small, hesitatant step of faith. As Doug himself said, "I simply took an old man to the bathroom. Anyone could have done that."

Going Deeper in the Word

A new beginning with the most important book you'll ever read awaits you. If you're satisfied to see the Book, the Bible, only through the eyes of the people you've met in these chapters, then don't read on.

If, however, these individuals, like Doug Nichols, have made you even the least bit curious to rediscover God's Word for yourself, then turn the page. The most significant chapter of your life is waiting to be written.

CHAPTER NINE

Making The Word Your Own

Twenty-Eight Days That Could Change Your Life

————∞————

Have you ever seen the monthly children's magazine *Highlights for Children?* For years, on the last page, was an illustration of an everyday scene with a headline that read, "In this picture find a rake, a guitar, a pencil, a. . . ." The challenge was to find each of the concealed objects. Each was usually so well disguised it finally made sense to me one day why *Highlights* seemed to be in every dentist's office in America. By the time you found all the hidden objects in the picture, the dentist was finally ready to see you!

The individuals in this book would make a poor *Highlights* "hidden object" lesson because, when you consider their remarkable stories, one thing cannot be concealed: the unmistakable power of God's Word to change lives. You have an opportunity now to experience this power in your own life—not just today, or this week, but for the rest of your life. By rekindling your love for God's Word, you can take hold of the greatest source of proven, timeless truth the world has ever known. In short: *The next twenty-eight days could be the most important time you ever spend in Scripture. Like the individuals in this book, you could be changed by the Book.*

Like Santos Galan of Mexico City and Nahum Gutierrez of Colima, Mexico, who were changed by God's Word, you could realize a new reason for living.

Like the Machiguengas of Peru who explored the Word, you could discover that the Bible really does speak your language.

Like Eugene Monakoff and Helene Vorobyova of Minsk, Belarus, who began examining the Word, you could be renewed by the Bible in those breakthrough moments when understanding and faith come together.

Like Yuri Gorban of Mariupal, Russia, who learned to depend daily on the Word, you could be pleasantly surprised at how the Bible reveals your true identity.

Like Rudy Cantuba, Reggie Opimiano, and Rudy Manzano of the Philippines, who received the Word others gave to them so effortlessly, you could be receiving the truth of the Bible even though you might be unwilling or unable.

Like four believers in China—Wang Cheng, Yang Meng, Wo San, and Su Han—you could come to cherish the Word by discovering how it can bring you unspeakable joy.

Like George Chen, who memorized portions of Scripture, you could experience the Word of life becoming life itself in you.

Indeed, like Doug Nichols, who patterned his life after the Word, you could discover that living the Bible truly does make all the difference in life.

Quality Time in the Word

You can know these realities for yourself by doing what each of these everyday Christians did—by spending consistent, quality time in God's Word. For you, that could be reading a chapter of Psalms or Proverbs each morning before you go off to work, or making Scripture a regular part of your lunch break. It may be relishing the silence after all the children have gone to bed to hear God's still, quiet voice speaking through the Old Testament, a Gospel, or a letter of Paul's.

Spending continual, quality time in Scripture is the key to rekindling your love for God's Word. It's the foundation of the plan I invite you to follow, a plan designed to help you experience the Bible in a new, revealing way that will draw you to a new, deeper, and lasting love of God.

In a nutshell, the plan is this: *To spend just twenty minutes a day, about two percent of your daily fourteen waking hours, in God's Word for the next twenty-eight days.*

Twenty minutes a day for four weeks. That's it.

Can it really make a difference? I know people who've asked this very question. Even though they had been distant from the Word, even indifferent to the Word, they made the time to read Scripture twenty or so minutes each day for a month. When they did, several things happened:

- They drew closer to God and experienced His power and presence in their daily lives.
- They found God speaking directly to their specific needs.
- They started applying Scripture to their lives.

Perhaps most remarkable of all is that these people, who either renewed their excitement for God's Word or discovered the Bible for the very first time, found themselves wanting to tell others about the things they were learning. One such person was the man who you met on the first page, Bruce Hurt.

Bruce Hurt's Indescribable Joy

For months, the Bible his wife gave Bruce for Christmas remained unopened and unread. Then, at the invitation of a fellow physician, Bruce reluctantly attended an outdoor barbecue hosted by Bible Study Fellowship. "That evening as the group studied the Gospel of John, I simply listened,"

Bruce recalled. "I couldn't say anything because I didn't know anything about the Bible. I was used to having people at the hospital look to me for knowledge. Now, I was the one who had all the questions. *I* was the patient in search of answers.

"When I got home that night I remembered scribbling down a verse someone had read at the barbecue: Jeremiah 15:16. I found the Bible Marty had given me for Christmas and looked up this verse: 'When your words came, I ate them; they were my joy and my heart's delight.'

"Over the next several days, as I began to read the Bible, the words of Jeremiah became true for me. For the first time in my life the Bible became real as I felt an indescribable joy of beginning to know God for the first time."

Over the years that have followed, Bruce has spread his joy to others. As a Sunday school teacher and Bible study leader at his church, Bruce Hurt has brought others into new, life-changing relationships with Jesus Christ.

Three Keys to Inductive Bible Study

The simplicity and power of the Word came to light for Bruce Hurt through a straightforward approach to Scripture known as the inductive Bible study method. Inductive Bible study is the heart of the twenty-eight-day approach to rekindling your love for God's Word. While some excellent study guides explain the method, here are three key principles that can maximize your time in Scripture:

1. Pray for the Holy Spirit to direct you. God has given all Christians His Spirit to be our teacher. As Jesus promised to His followers, "the Counselor, the Holy Spirit, whom the Father will send in my name, will teach you all things and will remind you of everything I have said to you" (John 14:26).

2. Read the passage to yourself. Observe What's going on. Who's speaking? What's being said? Once you see "the big picture," read the passage over several times. As you do:

- look for common words, names, and themes.
- write down your questions.
- note any words or phrases that seem unusual.

As you read and reflect, ask yourself three questions that can help make the passage real and relevant:

Look: What's going on in this passage?

Learn: What's God saying to me through these words?

Live: How can I live differently today as a result of God's Word living in me?

3. Act. Every passage of Scripture should lead you to ask yourself: What do these words mean to me? What am I going to feel, think, and believe because of this passage? Because God's Word is true, powerful, and practical, it can have a direct impact on you. But you need to act on it. By acting on God's Word, by making the Bible a way of life, you will discover more of the love, peace, and fellowship of Christ. Throughout the twenty-eight brief passages that follow, you'll be able to apply the specific Bible-study approaches that helped George Chen, Betty and Wayne Snell, and the others in this book deepen their love for God and His Word. Each of these insights, called "A Personal Word," offers the essence of these believers' personal discoveries to help transform your time in the Word from a mere reading exercise to a powerful encounter with the living God.

Before you begin your time in Scripture, I'd like to leave you with two stories that made me see just how accessible and precious the Bible can be for you and me.

Wisdom of a Cleaning Woman

Victor Nemtsev was an intelligent, educated, and successful man I met in Belarus in 1994. For a number of years he had been a university professor and the head of engineering and research at a large electronics factory in

Minsk. Over the months he became annoyed at a common cleaning woman in his office who often tried to talk to him and his colleagues about the gospel. "I just refused to talk to her," Victor told me, "but when I noticed that many of my coworkers were listening to her, I became angry.

"One day I was listening to her discussion with them and thought some of her arguments for Christianity were not too well stated. I decided to interject some of my own ideas to help her make more sense. This gave her the mistaken notion I was a Christian, so she gave me a New Testament!"

The things Victor began reading made him take the Bible more seriously than he ever imagined. Without abandoning his intellectual integrity, he came to accept the Bible's truth and decided to follow Jesus.

"It became very obvious to me that this was an incredibly complex book that answered all of the basic questions of life," he said. "At the same time, the very opposite was true; there was a beautiful simplicity to those answers that attracted me." Victor's insight led to a revealing thought: The "complex simplicity" of the Bible is that its truth is accessible to everyone. Regardless of your job title or religious background, whether you're a common cleaning woman or a brilliant university professor, you can know the one, true God as you come to know and love His Word.

Today, Victor Nemtsev epitomizes this truth. Today he directs the Bible League's work in Belarus and is pastor of a church in Minsk. A year after planting a new church with another pastor, they now have a worshiping congregation of 118 believers, two-thirds of whom are college or university educated.

Hands of a Martyr

Since the Bible can speak to life's questions with such simplicity and immediacy, it stands to reason that it would only become more important and precious to you over time. Indeed, my hope is that you and I would come to value the Word as much as a certain Chinese woman whose name I'll never know, yet whose story I'll never forget.

It was 1979. I was in Shanghai, China, promoting the work of the Bible League just a few years after many Chinese pastors and church leaders had been released from prison. For years public worship in China had been almost nonexistent. On this particular Sunday morning, however, the church service I attended was a sight to behold.

The sanctuary of the official government church was packed. The aisles were standing room only. I was prepared to stand with the Chinese believers, but our hosts made sure my American colleagues and I sat comfortably throughout the service. That's when I saw her.

She was in her mid-sixties, and she was seated next to me. The first thing I noticed was her hands. They were badly deformed. Though I tried not to stare, it was impossible to ignore that her fingers seemed frozen in a gnarled grip. Yet she held the bulletin, turning pages with her stiff fingers as freely as anyone else.

Another thing struck me that morning. Among the two thousand worshipers, I didn't see more than ten Bibles. For most of these Chinese believers, including the woman next to me, the only Scriptures they now had were the few verses listed in the bulletin. When the pastor read them out loud, everyone drew quiet in rapt attention.

Having been a missionary in Taiwan for a number of years, I spoke enough of the language to confirm a hunch I had about this woman. After the service we were walking out the door when I asked her, "Pardon me, but do you have a Bible?" She looked startled when I spoke to her. She was even more surprised that I had asked her about the Word.

"No, I do not have a Bible," she said politely.

"I have two Chinese Bibles in my hotel room," I replied. "I'm leaving Shanghai very early tomorrow morning. Would you like to come with me a few blocks to the hotel so you and a friend could each have your own copy?"

If that were the end of the story, I still would have never forgotten this woman because she looked so astonished and delighted. During the next several minutes as we walked to the hotel, I found out why she was deformed. Culturally, it would have been rude for me to ignore her hands. The polite thing was to acknowledge her condition yet not be offensive. I was careful how I phrased the question."Were you born with your hands the way they are today?" I asked.

"No," she replied. "I was born with normal hands. During the 1960s, as part of his Cultural Revolution, Mao Zedong gave his brutal police force, the Red Guards, complete legal authority to force their way into people's homes and take away all their possessions. One day, at the height of the Revolution, the Red Guards came to my door and forced their way inside. For being a Christian, I was called a 'revisionist,' the dirtiest word in the entire Communist vocabulary.

"The Red Guards began ransacking my tiny, two-room home. They turned over plants and stirred through chest drawers. They tore up everything in sight—books, photos, and other precious keepsakes. They were really looking for Scriptures and hymn books.

"They had ripped up the homes of so many believers that, by the time they reached me, they knew all the hiding places. The soldiers found my Bible beneath the ashes of my little cook stove. One guard held it in his hands, and as he turned in front of me to leave, I grabbed my Bible from him. He could have shoved me, knocked me down, or even killed me right then. The Red Guards could have easily pulled my hands apart and taken the Bible, but that wasn't their way.

"Instead, they laughed at me. They mocked and ridiculed me for being a Christian and owning a Bible. One would insult me, then another would spit on me. It went on like that for several minutes. 'Give up that book full of myths,' they said. 'Give up!'

"I looked at them and said, 'No, I cannot give up the Book, because in it is all I know of my Lord and Savior Jesus Christ.'

"That made them very angry. They stopped laughing, grabbed my arms, and led me outside. All I had to my name was the thin dress I wore and the Bible I still clutched in my hands. The Red Guards took me to a large, open area in the city. Under a cloudless sky and scorching sun they announced to the public what they were going to do. People flocked to the plaza where the Red Guards had pushed me up on a small pedestal two feet off the ground. The people swarmed around me. I knew the area well enough to know there had to be fifteen thousand people.

"In the open air, in full view of the crowd, the four Red Guards stripped me naked. All I had now was the Bible. I held it over my breasts and bowed my head. The soldiers thought I was ashamed. They didn't know I was praying to my Lord.

"The crowd took their cue from the Red Guard. For three hours, soldiers and citizens laughed at me and spit on me. Forward and back they surged like the tide, as the sun continued to beat down. When I thought I couldn't stand it any longer, the Red Guards stepped in. 'Give up that book full of myths!'

"I spoke as loud as I could. 'No, I cannot give up the Book, because in it is all that I know of my Lord and Savior Jesus Christ.' The soldiers became angrier than before. They pushed me down from the pedestal, then laid me on my stomach in the street. To hold onto the Bible, I stretched my arms in front.

"Then, one of the guards put his foot on the back of my head, and the other three began to beat my hands with lead pipes. I never felt such pain. They hit me again and again until my hands were so weak I had no feeling. I could no longer hold onto the Bible. It slipped from my hands and fell in the dirt, as the crowd cheered."

At that moment in her story, as we stood outside my hotel, the woman raised her gnarled hands and said, "That day, laying naked and facedown, no longer able to feel my hands, was the last time I held a copy of God's Word."

It took me less than five minutes, a short, round-trip elevator ride up to my room and back, to gather the two Chinese Bibles I had. I brought them to the woman, and, when no one was looking, I put them in her clawed hands. She looked at me in silence, unable to speak as tears rolled down her cheeks. Then, she turned and walked down the sidewalk, back into the noontime sea of people.

That was the first and last time I ever saw her. Yet her gratefulness for the Word is something I'll never forget. Today, whenever I think of her, whenever I see her clutching the Bible, I see why she would never want to let go. That day in Shanghai I saw how precious the Word of God can be to someone. That day I saw how much the Word can mean to people everywhere, people in my country, people like you and me who have God's perfect, revealed, and life-changing message right within our reach.

Days 1–14: Renewing Your Love for Jesus Christ

All of the true tories in this book, from the near-tragedy of Santos Galan to the tears of a Chinese woman, are designed to draw you closer to God's story, to His Word, the Bible. There is only one way I know to rekindle your love for this greatest of all life-changing books, *and that is to read it.*

If you're already reading the Bible regularly, then you know the joy His Word can bring; but if the Bible has not been part of your daily pattern, and you would truly like to rekindle your love for a book that can seem so overwhelming, here is an invitation that could change your life.

Beginning today, for the next four weeks I ask you to invest twenty minutes a day to read and reflect on God's Word. That's it.

Twenty minutes a day for four weeks.

Twenty minutes at the breakfast table.

Or during a break in-between class.

At lunch.

After washing the dishes.

Or before you go to bed.

Twenty private, peaceful minutes with the living Lord who put His love to you in writing.

The God who transformed Victor Nemsev and who sustained a faithful Chinese woman wants to touch you, today, with the most precious resource you will ever lay your hands on.

Before you are twenty-eight of the most revealing passages in all of Scripture: Fourteen brief passages will renew your love for Jesus, and fourteen more will revive your love for the Old Testament.

Some passages feature "A Personal Word," actual words from some of the faithful, inspiring Christians you have read about that can show you how to get more out of your daily reading.

Each passage gives you the opportunity to ask three questions that can take you closer to the actual text and closer to God:

1. What's going on in the passage?
2. What might God be saying to you through these words?
3. How can you live differently, today, as a result of God's Word living in you?

As you read the Word and ask the Holy Spirit to guide you, remember this: *The greatest truth you will ever know is waiting to be found in God's Word. Read the Word and you will come to love the Word—and love the One who loves you unconditionally.*

May everything you have read in this book lead you to *the* Book and the Lord who is working in you, calling you to Himself, even now.

Day 1: Luke 1—Preparing for Jesus' Arrival
A Personal Word

"If you're plunging into the Bible for the first time, you're like the person who's familiar with Scripture yet desires the words to be new. That newness isn't found so much in the 'big picture' but in the details many tend to overlook.

"The overlooked details of Scripture not only help make the Scripture new for us, they also draw us into the Scripture itself by showing us what we know and don't know about characters."—Eugene Monakoff and Helene Vorobyova, chapter 3

What overlooked details can you find in Zechariah, Mary, and Elizabeth's story that would help you step into their shoes so you could experience a sense of what they felt leading up to Jesus' birth?

Look. What's going on in this passage?

_____

_____

_____

_____

_____

_____

Learn. What's God saying to me through these words?

_____

_____

_____

_____

_____

Live. How can I live differently today as a result of God's Word living in me?

_____
_____
_____
_____
_____
_____
_____

Day 2: Luke 2—The Story of Jesus' Birth

Look. What's going on in this passage?

_____
_____
_____
_____
_____
_____

Learn. What's God saying to me through these words?

_____
_____
_____
_____
_____
_____

Live. How can I live differently today as a result of God's Word living in me?

_____
_____
_____
_____
_____

Day 3: Mark 1—The Beginning of Jesus' Ministry

Look. What's going on in this passage?

_____
_____
_____
_____
_____
_____
_____

Learn. What's God saying to me through these words?

_____
_____
_____
_____
_____
_____

Live. How can I live differently today as a result of God's Word living in me?

_____
_____
_____
_____
_____
_____

Day 4: Mark 9—A Day in the Life of Jesus

Look. What's going on in this passage?

_____
_____
_____
_____
_____

Learn.   What's God saying to me through these words?

_____
_____
_____
_____
_____
_____

Live.   How can I live differently today as a result of God's Word living in me?

_____
_____
_____
_____
_____
_____

Day 5: Matthew 5—The Sermon on the Mount
A Personal Word

> "Please leave this book with me so I can read it," Su Han said.
>
> The woman took the book from her lap and put it on the table. "I can leave this with you for one week," she said. . . . That night, after the woman left, Su Han did something so natural she thought nothing of it. She took the only piece of paper and pencil she could find and began copying the words of this book called "The New Testament." If she couldn't keep the book, she thought, at least she could find a way to hold on to the words.— chapter 6

If you were able to keep the Sermon on the Mount for only twenty minutes, what portions of it would you copy for yourself? Considering what happened to Su Han, can you give any reason why it wouldn't be worthwhile to write out these verses right now?

Look. What's going on in this passage?

_____
_____
_____
_____
_____
_____

Learn. What's God saying to me through these words?

_____
_____
_____
_____
_____

Live. How can I live differently today as a result of God's Word living in me?

_____
_____
_____
_____
_____
_____

Day 6: Matthew 6—The Sermon on the Mount

Look. What's going on in this passage?

_____
_____
_____

_____

_____

_____

_____

Learn. What's God saying to me through these words?

_____

_____

_____

_____

_____

_____

Live. How can I live differently today as a result of God's Word living in me?

_____

_____

_____

_____

_____

_____

Day 7: Luke 15—The Parables of Jesus

Look. What's going on in this passage?

_____

_____

_____

_____

_____

Learn. What's God saying to me through these words?

_____

_____

_____

_____
_____
_____

Live. How can I live differently today as a result of
God's Word living in me?

_____
_____
_____
_____
_____
_____
_____

Day 8: John 3—A Conversation with Jesus
A Personal Word

By memorizing portions of the Word, George not only
embraced the Word as a trusted guide for daily living, he
experienced the Word as life *itself.*—chapter 7

If you could memorize one passage of five to ten verses
(other than John 3:16) within the next four weeks, which
of the twenty-eight passages in this plan would you
choose?

Look. What's going on in this passage?

_____
_____
_____
_____
_____
_____

Learn. What's God saying to me through these words?

_____

_____

_____

_____

_____

_____

Live. How can I live differently today as a result of God's Word living in me?

_____

_____

_____

_____

_____

_____

Day 9: John 14—Jesus' Final Instructions

Look. What's going on in this passage?

_____

_____

_____

_____

_____

_____

Learn. What's God saying to me through these words?

_____

_____

_____

_____

_____

Live. How can I live differently today as a result of
God's Word living in me?

_____

_____

_____

_____

_____

_____

_____

_____

Day 10: John 17—Jesus' Prayer for His Disciples
A Personal Word

> "Everything I have learned about my true worth as a
> person, my identity in the Lord, has come from reading
> the Bible on a daily basis. All that I read in the Bible, all
> that I know myself to be true has deepened over time not
> because I have kept these truths to myself, *but because
> I have shared them with others.*"—Yuri Gorban,
> chapter 4

Jesus' prayer to His heavenly Father reveals that one's
true worth is rooted in a personal relationship with God. Of
the twenty-six verses in this passage, which of Jesus'
words are so revealing that you would find it hard not to
share them with others?

Look. What's going on in this passage?

_____

_____

_____

_____

_____

Learn. What's God saying to me through these words?

_____

_____

_____

_____

_____

_____

_____

Live. How can I live differently today as a result of God's Word living in me?

_____

_____

_____

_____

_____

_____

Day 11: Matthew 26—Betrayal and Arrest

Look. What's going on in this passage?

_____

_____

_____

_____

_____

_____

Learn. What's God saying to me through these words?

_____

_____

_____

_____

_____

_____

Live. How can I live differently today as a result of God's Word living in me?

_____

_____

_____

_____

_____

_____

Day 12: Matthew 27—Jesus' Execution on a Cross
A Personal Word

> In his hour of greatest need, Reggie [Opimiano] received the truth and power of Scripture because his wife knew how to pray the Word.—chapter 5

In His hour of greatest need, Jesus cried out to His Father. What does that say to you about God's accessibility and presence when you are faced with an impossible situation?

Look. What's going on in this passage?

_____

_____

_____

_____

_____

_____

Learn. What's God saying to me through these words?

_____

_____

_____

_____

_____

_____

Live. How can I live differently today as a result of God's Word living in me?

_____

_____

_____

_____

_____

Day 13: John 20—Resurrection

Look. What's going on in this passage?

_____

_____

_____

_____

_____

Learn. What's God saying to me through these words?

_____

_____

_____

_____

_____

Live. How can I live differently today as a result of God's Word living in me?

_____

_____

_____

_____

_____

_____

_____

Day 14: Luke 24—Jesus' Appearance after Resurrection
A Personal Word

> "Even though you may not always understand what
> you read, the Bible will speak powerfully and directly to
> what you need."—Nahum Gutierrez, chapter 1

Imagine you were one of the people in Luke 24 who met
Jesus after His resurrection. What things would you have
not understood? What things do you still not understand?
How would you express these questions to God in a prayer
for what you need from His Word?

Look. What's going on in this passage?

_____

_____

_____

_____

_____

_____

_____

Learn. What's God saying to me through these words?

_____

_____

_____

_____

_____

Live. How can I live differently today as a result of God's Word living in me?

_____

_____

_____

_____

_____

_____

_____

Days 15–28: Renewing Your Love for the Old Testament
Day 15: Genesis 1—The Story of Creation

Look. What's going on in this passage?

_____

_____

_____

_____

_____

_____

_____

Learn. What's God saying to me through these words?

_____

_____

_____

_____

_____

Live. How can I live differently today as a result of God's Word living in me?

_____

_____

_____

_____
_____
_____
_____

Day 16: Genesis 3—The Origin of Sin

Look. What's going on in this passage?

_____
_____
_____
_____
_____
_____

Learn. What's God saying to me through these words?

_____
_____
_____
_____
_____
_____
_____
_____

Live. How can I live differently today as a result of God's Word living in me?

_____
_____
_____
_____
_____
_____
_____

Day 17: Genesis 22—Abraham and Isaac
A Personal Word

> "Lord, I don't know how to obey You."
> "Lord, I don't know if I can trust You."
> "Lord, I'm not sure I have what it takes to believe in You."—Doug Nichols, chapter 8

These were the questions that led up to Doug acting on the Word. As you look at Abraham's challenge to obey, trust, and believe, how is God challenging you to do the same by living His Word today?

Look.   What's going on in this passage?

_____
_____
_____
_____
_____
_____
_____

Learn.   What's God saying to me through these words?

_____
_____
_____
_____
_____
_____

Live.   How can I live differently today as a result of God's Word living in me?

_____
_____
_____
_____

_____

_____

_____

Day 18: Exodus 3—Moses' Encounter with God

Look. What's going on in this passage?

_____

_____

_____

_____

_____

_____

Learn. What's God saying to me through these words?

_____

_____

_____

_____

_____

Live. How can I live differently today as a result of God's Word living in me?

_____

_____

_____

_____

_____

_____

Day 19: Exodus 20—The Gift of the Ten Commandments
A Personal Word

One of the simplest, most direct ways to receive the Word and know its power, as Rudy Cantuba discovered, is to read it whenever it's within your reach.

Rudy received the Word because a friend simply gave him his own copy of the Bible.—chapter 5

Do you know someone who could benefit from receiving their own copy of the Word? How would a Bible help this person see that God is not just One who "lays down the Law"?

Look. What's going on in this passage?

_____
_____
_____
_____
_____
_____
_____

Learn. What's God saying to me through these words?

_____
_____
_____
_____
_____
_____

Live. How can I live differently today as a result of God's Word living in me?

_____
_____
_____

_____

_____

_____

_____

Day 20: 1 Samuel 17—David and Goliath

Look. What's going on in this passage?

_____

_____

_____

_____

_____

_____

Learn. What's God saying to me through these words?

_____

_____

_____

_____

_____

Live. How can I live differently today as a result of God's Word living in me?

_____

_____

_____

_____

_____

Day 21: 2 Samuel 11—David and Bathsheba

Look. What's going on in this passage?

_____

_____

_____

_____

_____

_____

Learn. What's God saying to me through these words?

_____

_____

_____

_____

_____

_____

Live. How can I live differently today as a result of God's Word living in me?

_____

_____

_____

_____

_____

Day 22: 2 Samuel 12—Nathan's Rebuke of the King

Look. What's going on in this passage?

_____

_____

_____

_____

_____

_____
_____

Learn.   What's God saying to me through these words?

_____
_____
_____
_____
_____
_____

Live.   How can I live differently today as a result of God's Word living in me?

_____
_____
_____
_____
_____
_____

Day 23: 1 Kings 18—Elijah and the Prophets of Baal

Look.   What's going on in this passage?

_____
_____
_____
_____
_____
_____

Learn.   What's God saying to me through these words?

_____
_____
_____
_____
_____

_____

_____

Live. How can I live differently today as a result of God's Word living in me?

_____

_____

_____

_____

_____

_____

_____

Day 24: Job 38—God's Answer to Job

A Personal Word

> What allowed the Machiguengas to know the God who spoke their language was that they came to Scripture as strangers to the truth. Their lack of knowledge wasn't a barrier, but rather an open gate, through which the Holy Spirit flowed.—chapter 4

If you've ever come to Scripture with a lack of knowledge and understanding about human suffering, you're in good company—with Job. As you read the Lord's response to His faithful servant, be open to how the Holy Spirit could speak to you about what good can come out of suffering.

Look. What's going on in this passage?

_____

_____

_____

_____

_____

_____

Learn. What's God saying to me through these words?

_____
_____
_____
_____
_____
_____
_____

Live. How can I live differently today as a result of God's Word living in me?

_____
_____
_____
_____
_____
_____

Day 25: Psalm 51—A Classic Confession
A Personal Word

By receiving the Word, Carmen knew how to pray the Word. By praying the Word, Carmen saw her husband come to renewed faith. And by receiving the Word, Reggie was able to receive and extend the same forgiveness Christ had shown him; he was able to live the Word: "Forgive as the Lord forgave you" (Col. 3:13).—chapter 5

What does God want you to receive in David's confession of Psalm 51?

Look. What's going on in this passage?

_____
_____

_____

_____

_____

_____

Learn. What's God saying to me through these words?

_____

_____

_____

_____

_____

_____

Live. How can I live differently today as a result of God's Word living in me?

_____

_____

_____

_____

_____

_____

Day 26: Isaiah 40—Words of Comfort from God
A Personal Word

Because someone spoke the written Word, Rudy Manzano was able to receive the Living Word. Only because of this was Rudy able to turn to the Word when he needed it the most.—chapter 5

What words in Isaiah speak to you the loudest?

Look. What's going on in this passage?

_____

_____

_____
_____
_____
_____
_____

Learn.   What's God saying to me through these words?

_____
_____
_____
_____
_____
_____

Live.   How can I live differently today as a result of God's Word living in me?

_____
_____
_____
_____
_____
_____

Day 27: Daniel 6—Daniel and the Lions

Look.   What's going on in this passage?

_____
_____
_____
_____
_____

Learn.   What's God saying to me through these words?

_____
_____

_____

_____

_____

_____

_____

Live. How can I live differently today as a result of
God's Word living in me?

_____

_____

_____

_____

_____

_____

Day 28: Amos 4—A Prophet's Stern Warning

Look. What's going on in this passage?

_____

_____

_____

_____

_____

_____

Learn. What's God saying to me through these words?

_____

_____

_____

_____

_____

_____

Live. How can I live differently today as a result of God's Word living in me?

_____

_____

_____

_____

_____

_____

_____

CHAPTER TEN

A New Discovery Each Day

Rekindling your love for God's Word can be a daily discovery that lasts a lifetime. Each time you read, study, and reflect on Scripture, it can be a new opportunity to experience God—His power, wisdom, faithfulness, and love. That discovery process can begin today with either one of two extended reading plans designed to ground you in God's Word.

Track 1: Every Book in the Bible

Time commitment: Six months

Goal: To gain an overview of the entire Bible

Track 1 includes 182 of the 1,189 chapters of the Bible. As you'll discover, some well-known sections of Scripture are not represented. In some cases, like Leviticus, for example, you'll only read one chapter.

The chapters were selected because, generally speaking, they're understandable and don't require a commentary. Taken together, they provide a good foundation of biblical understanding.

Reading suggestion: If you miss a few days, don't worry. Just resume reading when you can, about a chapter a day. In 180 days, you'll have read from every book in the Bible.

Genesis	___1	___2	___3	___4
	___7	___8	___15	___19
	___22	___27	___28	___37
	___41	___45		

Exodus	___3 ___32	___10–11 ___14	___20
Leviticus	___26		
Numbers	___11	___14	
Deuteronomy	___4	___8	___28
Joshua	___2	___6	___7 ___24
Judges	___6	___7	___16
Ruth	___1		
1 Samuel	___3	___16	___17
2 Samuel	___6	___11	___12
1 Kings	___3	___8	___17 ___18
2 Kings	___5	___17	___22
1 Chronicles	___17		
2 Chronicles	___20	___30	___32
Ezra	___3		
Nehemiah	___2	___8	
Esther	___4		
Job	___1–2	___38	___42
Psalms	___9 ___84	___23 ___103	___27 ___51 ___139
Proverbs	___4	___10	
Ecclesiastes	___3		
Song of Solomon	___2		

Isaiah	___6	___25	___40	___52
	___53	___55		
Jeremiah	___2	___15	___31	___38
Lamentations	___3			
Ezekiel	___1	___2–3	___4	___37
Daniel	___1	___3	___5	___6
Hosea	___2–3	___11		
Joel	___2			
Amos	___4			
Obadiah	___ Obadiah			
Jonah	___3–4			
Micah	___6			
Nahum	___1			
Habakkuk	___1			
Zephaniah	___3			
Haggai	___1			
Zechariah	___8			
Malachi	___3			
Matthew	___5	___6	___13	___19
	___26	___27	___28	
Mark	___1	___2	___3	___4
	___5	___6	___7	___8
	___9	___10	___11	___12
	___13	___14	___15–16	

Luke	___1	___2	___10	___12
	___15	___16	___18	___24
John	___3	___6	___10	___14
	___15	___16	___17	___20
Acts	___1	___2	___5	___9
	___16	___17	___26	___27
	___28			
Romans	___3	___7	___8	___12
1 Corinthians	___13	___15		
2 Corinthians	___4	___12		
Galatians	___3			
Ephesians	___2	___3		
Philippians	___2			
Colossians	___1			
1 Thessalonians	___3–4			
2 Thessalonians	___2			
1 Timothy	___1			
2 Timothy	___2			
Titus	___2			
Philemon	___Philemon			
Hebrews	___2	___11	___12	
James	___1			
1 Peter	___1			
2 Peter	___1			

1 John	___3		
2 and 3 John	___2, 3 John		
Jude	___Jude		
Revelation	___1	___12	___21

Track 2: Every Word of the Bible

Time commitment: Three years
Goal: To read the entire Bible

Track 2 takes you completely through the Bible, reading every word. Typical yearly reading plans require you to read at least three chapters a day. Many people, however, find such a pace unrealistic and discouraging. Therefore, Track 2 requires only one chapter of reading a day. (Some short chapters have been combined, so occasionally you'll read two brief chapters a day.)

Track 2 alternates between the Old and New Testaments. This mix provides variety and reduces the possibility of reading fatigue.

Genesis	___1	___2	___3	___4
	___5	___6	___7	___8
	___9	___10–11	___12	___13
	___14	___15	___16	___17
	___18	___19	___20	___21
	___22	___23	___24	___25
	___26	___27	___28	___29
	___30	___31	___32	___33
	___34	___35	___36	___37
	___38	___39	___40	___41
	___42	___43	___44	___45
	___46	___47	___48	___49
	___50			

Matthew 1–9	__1	__2	__3	__4
	__5	__6	__7	__8
	__9			

Exodus	__1	__2	__3–4	__5
	__6	__7	__8	__9
	__10–11	__12	__13	__14
	__15	__16	__17	__18
	__19	__20	__21	__22
	__23	__24	__25	__26
	__27	__28	__29	__30
	__31	__32	__33	__34
	__35	__36	__37	__38
	__39	__40		

Matthew 10–20	__10	__11	__12	__13
	__14	__15	__16	__17
	__18	__19	__20	

Leviticus 1–14	__1	__2	__3	__4
	__5	__6	__7	__8
	__9	__10	__11–12	__13
	__14			

Matthew 21–28	__21	__22	__23	__24
	__25	__26	__27	__28

Leviticus 15–27	__15–16	__17	__18	__19
	__20	__21	__22	__23
	__24	__25	__26	__27

Mark 1–8	__1	__2	__3	__4
	__5	__6	__7	__8

Numbers	___1–2	___3	___4	___5
	___6	___7	___8	___9
	___10	___11	___12	___13
	___14	___15	___16	___17
	___18	___19	___20	___21
	___22	___23	___24	___25
	___26	___27	___28	___29
	___30	___31	___32	___33
	___34	___35	___36	

Mark 9–16	___9	___10	___11	___12
	___13	___14	___15–16	

Deuteronomy 1–17	___1	___2	___3	___4
	___5	___6	___7	___8
	___9	___10	___11	___12
	___13	___14	___15	___16
	___17			

Luke 1–8	___1	___2	___3	___4
	___5	___6	___7	___8

Deuteronomy 18–34	___18	___19	___20	___21
	___22	___23	___24	___25
	___26	___27	___28	___29
	___30	___31	___32	___33
	___34			

Luke 9–16	___9	___10	___11	___12
	___13	___14	___15	___16

Joshua	___1	___2	___3	___4
	___5	___6	___7	___8
	___9	___10	___11	___12–13
	___14–15	___16–17	___18	___19
	___20	___21	___22	___23
	___24			

Luke 17–24	__17	__18	__19	__20
	__21	__22	__23	__24
Judges	__1	__2	__3	__4
	__5	__6	__7	__8
	__9	__10	__11	__12
	__13	__14	__15	__16
	__17	__18	__19	__20–21
John 1–7	__1	__2	__3	__4
	__5	__6	__7	
Ruth	__1	__2	__3	__4
1 Samuel 1–15	__1	__2	__3	__4
	__5	__6	__7	__8
	__9	__10	__11–12	__13
	__14	__15		
John 8–14	__8	__9	__10	__11
	__12	__13	__14	
1 Samuel 16–31	__16	__17	__18	__19
	__20	__21	__22	__23
	__24	__25	__26	__27
	__28	__29	__30	__31
John 15–21	__15–16	__17	__18	__19
	__20	__21		
2 Samuel	__1	__2	__3	__4
	__5	__6	__7	__8
	__9	__10	__11	__12
	__13	__14	__15	__16
	__17	__18	__19	__20
	__21	__22	__23	__24
Acts 1–7	__1	__2	__3	__4
	__5	__6	__7	

Acts 8–14	__8	__9	__10	__11
	__12	__13	__14	

1 Kings 1–11	__1	__2	__3	__4
	__5	__6	__7	__8
	__9	__10	__11	

1 Kings 12–22	__12	__13	__14	__15
	__16	__17	__18	__19
	__20	__21	__22	

Acts 15–21	__15	__16	__17	__18
	__19	__20	__21	

2 Kings	__1	__2	__3	__4
	__5	__6	__7	__8
	__9	__10	__11	__12
	__13	__14	__15	__16
	__17	__18	__19	__20
	__21	__22	__23	__24
	__25			

Acts 22–28	__22	__23	__24	__25
	__26	__27	__28	

1 Chronicles 1–14	__1–9	__10	__11	__12
	__13	__14		

Romans 1–8	__1	__2	__3	__4
	__5	__6	__7	__8

1 Chronicles 15–29	__15	__16	__17	__18
	__19	__20	__21	__22
	__23	__24	__25	__26
	__27	__28	__29	

Romans 9–16	__9	__10	__11	__12
	__13	__14	__15	__16

2 Chronicles 1–18   ___1   ___2   ___3   ___4
                     ___5   ___6   ___7   ___8
                     ___9   ___10   ___11   ___12
                     ___13   ___14   ___15   ___16
                     ___17   ___18

1 Corinthians 1–9   ___1   ___2   ___3   ___4
                     ___5   ___6   ___7   ___8
                     ___9

2 Chronicles 19–36   ___19   ___20   ___21   ___22
                     ___23   ___24   ___25   ___26
                     ___27   ___28   ___29   ___30
                     ___31   ___32   ___33   ___34
                     ___35   ___36

1 Corinthians 10–16 ___10   ___11   ___12   ___13
                     ___14   ___15   ___16

Ezra   ___1–2   ___3   ___4   ___5
                     ___6   ___7   ___8   ___9
                     ___10

Nehemiah   ___1–2   ___3   ___4   ___5
                     ___6   ___7   ___8   ___9
                     ___10   ___11   ___12   ___13

2 Corinthians   ___1   ___2–3   ___4   ___5
                     ___6   ___7   ___8–9   ___10
                     ___11   ___12–13

Esther   ___1   ___2   ___3   ___4
                     ___5   ___6–7   ___8   ___9–10

Job 1–21   ___1   ___2   ___3   ___4
                     ___5   ___6   ___7   ___8
                     ___9   ___10   ___11   ___12
                     ___13   ___14   ___15   ___16
                     ___17   ___18   ___19   ___20
                     ___21

Galatians	__1	__2	__3	__4
	__5–6			

Job 22–42	__22	__23	__24	__25
	__26	__27	__28	__29
	__30	__31	__32	__33
	__34	__35	__36	__37
	__38	__39	__40	__41
	__42			

Ephesians	__1	__2	__3	__4
	__5	__6		

Psalms 1–40	__1	__2	__3	__4
	__5	__6	__7	__8
	__9	__10	__11	__12
	__13	__14	__15	__16
	__17	__18	__19	__20
	__21	__22	__23	__24
	__25	__26	__27	__28
	__29	__30	__31	__32
	__33	__34	__35	__36
	__37	__38	__39	__40

Philippians	__1	__2	__3	__4

Psalms 41–80	__41	__42–43	__44	__45
	__46–47	__48	__49	__50
	__51	__52	__53–54	__55
	__56	__57	__58	__59
	__60–61	__62	__63–64	__65
	__66	__67	__68	__69
	__70	__71	__72	__73
	__74	__75	__76	__77
	__78	__79	__80	

Colossians	__1	__2	__3	__4

Psalms 81–121   ___81   ___82
                     ___83   ___84
                     ___85   ___86
                     ___87   ___88
                     ___89   ___90–91
                     ___92–93   ___94
                     ___95   ___96
                     ___97   ___98–99
                     ___100–101   ___102
                     ___103   ___104
                     ___105   ___106
                     ___107   ___108
                     ___109   ___110–111
                     ___112–113   ___114
                     ___115   ___116–117
                     ___118   ___119:1–48
                     ___119:49–96   ___119:97–144
                     ___119:145–176   ___120–121

1 Thessalonians   ___1–2   ___3–4   ___5

2 Thessalonians   ___1–2   ___3

Psalms 122–150   ___122–123   ___124–125
                     ___126–128   ___129–130
                     ___131–132   ___133–134
                     ___135   ___136
                     ___137–138   ___139
                     ___140   ___141–142
                     ___143   ___144
                     ___145   ___146
                     ___147   ___148
                     ___149–150

Proverbs	__1	__2	__3	__4
	__5	__6	__7	__8
	__9	__10	__11	__12
	__13	__14	__15	__16
	__17	__18	__19	__20
	__21	__22	__23	__24
	__25	__26	__27	__28
	__29	__30	__31	
1 Timothy	__1–2	__3–4	__5	__6
Ecclesiastes	__1	__2	__3	__4
	__5	__6	__7	__8
	__9	__10	__11	__12
Song of Solomon	__1	__2	__3	__4
	__5	__6	__7	__8
2 Timothy	__1	__2	__3	__4
Isaiah 1–36	__1	__2	__3	__4
	__5	__6	__7	__8
	__9	__10	__11	__12
	__13	__14	__15	__16
	__17	__18	__19–20	__21
	__22	__23	__24	__25
	__26	__27	__28	__29
	__30	__31	__32	__33
	__34	__35	__36	
Titus	__1	__2–3		

Isaiah 37–66	___37	___38–39	___40	___41
	___42	___43	___44	___45
	___46	___47	___48	___49
	___50	___51	___52	___53
	___54	___55	___56	___57
	___58	___59	___60	___61
	___62	___63	___64	___65
	___66			

Philemon	___Philemon			

Jeremiah 1–26	___1	___2	___3	___4
	___5	___6	___7	___8
	___9	___10	___11	___12
	___13	___14	___15	___16
	___17	___18	___19	___20
	___21	___22	___23	___24
	___25	___26		

Hebrews 1–7	___1	___2	___3–4	___5–6
	___7			

Jeremiah 27–52	___27	___28	___29	___30
	___31	___32	___33	___34
	___35	___36	___37	___38
	___39	___40	___41	___42
	___43	___44–45	___46	___47
	___48	___49	___50	___51
	___52			

Hebrews 8–13	___8	___9	___10	___11
	___12	___13		

Lamentations	___1	___2	___3	___4
	___5			

Ezekiel 1–24	___1	___2–3	___4	___5
	___6	___7	___8	___9
	___10	___11	___12	___13
	___14	___15	___16	___17
	___18	___19	___20	___21
	___22	___23	___24	

James	___1	___2	___3–4	___5

Ezekiel 25–48	___25	___26	___27	___28
	___29	___30	___31	___32
	___33	___34	___35	___36
	___37	___38	___39	___40
	___41	___42	___43	___44
	___45	___46	___47	___48

1 Peter	___1	___2	___3	___4–5

Daniel	___1	___2	___3	___4
	___5	___6	___7	___8
	___9	___10	___11	___12

2 Peter	___1	___2	___3

Hosea	___1	___2–3	___4	___5
	___6–7	___8	___9	___10
	___11–12	___13–14		

1 John	___1–2	___3	___4	___5

Joel	___1	___2	___3

Amos	___1	___2	___3	___4
	___5	___6	___7	___8
	___9			

Obadiah	___Obadiah

Jonah	___1–2	___3–4

2 and 3 John	___ 2 and 3 John

Micah	__1	__2	__3	__4
	__5	__6	__7	

Nahum	__1	__2	__3

Jude	__Jude

Habakkuk	__1	__2	__3

Zephaniah	__1	__2	__3

Revelation 1–7	__1	__2	__3	__4–5
	__6	__7		

Haggai	__1	__2

Revelation 8–14	__8	__9	__10–11	__12
	__13	__14		

Zechariah	__1	__2–3	__4–5	__6
	__7	__8	__9	__10
	__11	__12–13	__14	

Malachi	__1	__2	__3–4

Revelation 15–22	__15–16	__17	__18	__19
	__20	__21	__22	